PRAISE FOR MUMIA ABU-JAMAL

"Abu-Jamal's writing tends to be forceful, outraged, and humorous, but he also engages in the bombastic approaches of another era. . . . The author offers powerful columns on diverse subjects ranging from the plight of black farmers to the crushing of dissent after 9/11. Some remain all too relevant—e.g., those decrying systemic police brutality as seen in flashpoints from Rodney King to Ferguson or the rise of racial disparities in drug sentencing. Abu-Jamal meditates on central figures in the black political narrative, ranging from Dr. Martin Luther King Jr. to Trayvon Martin. . . . These topical essays [from 1982 to 2014] testify to the effects of incarceration on mind and spirit. While his prose has sharpened over time, Abu-Jamal remains enraged and pessimistic about an America that, in his view, remains wholly corrupt: '[Blacks] know from bitter experience that while Americans may say one thing, they mean something quite different.'"

—*Kirkus Reviews* for *Writing on the Wall*

"Hope and the seeds of revolution can come from the depths of isolation. Writing from his cell on death row, where he was held in solitary confinement for nearly 30 years, Abu-Jamal has long been a loud and clear voice for all who suffer injustice, racism, and poverty. Edited by [Johanna] Fernández, this selection of 100 previously unpublished essays includes a foreword by Cornel West."

—Evan Karp, *SF Weekly* for *Writing on the Wall*

"The power of his voice is rooted in his defiance of those determined to silence him. Magically, Mumia's words are clarified, purified by the toxic strata of resistance they must penetrate to reach us. Like the blues. Like jazz."

—John Edgar Wideman

"Mumia refuses to allow his spirit to be broken by the forces of injustice; his language glows with an affirming flame."

—Jonathon Kozol

HAVE BLACK LIVES EVER MATTERED?

HAVE BLACK LIVES EVER MATTERED?

Mumia Abu-Jamal

City Lights Books | Open Media Series

Open Media Series editor: Greg Ruggiero

Library of Congress Cataloging-in-Publication Data
on file

ISBN: 9780872867383 (paperbound), 9780872867390 (ebook)

City Lights Books are published at the City Lights Bookstore
261 Columbus Avenue, San Francisco, CA 94133
www.citylights.com

CONTENTS

DEDICATION

To the Nameless Ones, those valiant souls who fought for Freedom their whole lives long, and never lived to taste its intoxicating flavor; to the sons and daughters of Africa who lived in this strange and cruel land, yet dreamed of brighter tomorrows.

To Lydia Umyemi Wallace Barashango and her devoted husband, Rev. Dr. Ishakamusa Barashango, the renowned brilliant nationalist scholar and teacher; to the beautiful Bev Africa; to Samiya Hamida Abdullah, whose life was like a brilliant shooting star, who dazzled us all, before falling back into the river of Eternity: gone, but never forgotten, for in our hearts, in our being, she shines still.

To Ron "The Flame," Basil Ali Abu-Jaleel, a brother loved despite the distance of time and space.

To souls who shone brightly, and were dulled by American hate; to those who struggle still; to the youth of America who dared to march, to yell, to stand on the simple Principle that Black Lives Matter, I hereby dedicate this work.

Spring *is* coming,

—Mumia Abu-Jamal

HAVE BLACK LIVES EVER MATTERED?

An Introduction

Does the title of this work seem provocative? If so, then good. That's how it's intended to be. For if the question is provocative, then what of the answer? Is not the answer, no matter how damning, far more provocative? And yet, who dares answer in any way other than the negative?

There is an old axiom, especially among journalists and journalism professors, that "today's newspapers are the first draft of history." Like most axioms, they hold a kernel of truth, but there is more.

Here is another axiom: "History is written by the victors."

The words printed here were not written by a victor, but by one who has seen and sensed what was happening on the other side of a prison wall, who seeks to convey those impressions with truth, and who has often done so several times a week.

In a sense, the impressions recorded in the pages ahead are a form of history—Black history—recorded during a particular passage of time. During this particular period we experienced the greatest economic disaster since the Great Depression of the 1930s, the cultural dominance of hip-hop, the nation's fever over mass incarceration, the Obama presidency, the spread of the Black Lives Matter movement, and the unexpected onset of the Donald J. Trump era.

True history—what Howard Zinn called "the people's history"—is the one that ordinary people create through their everyday struggles. And yet for Blacks, much that never makes it to the newspapers—or, if so, only in a distorted form—still leaves scars in the mind, evidence of traumas sustained from simply *existing* as a Black person in the United States of America.

The pages ahead reflect the people's struggles in the invisible sectors of American society, sectors which, by a terrible necessity, are populated largely by Blacks, Latinos, immigrants, the incarcerated, and those with little income. The pages ahead are also, by equal necessity, reflections of insurgent, emergent, radical, and revolutionary aspiration, thinking, and living. For from oppression comes solidarity, resistance, rebellion, and change.

National movements like Black Lives Matter are manifestations of such solidarity and resistance, and give voice to the eruption of outrage, angst, hopes, and insurgent protest provoked by each new killing. That such a movement was brought into being by three young women of color—Patrisse Cullors, Opal Tometi, and Alicia Garza—is telling, for throughout American history we have seen how the dedicated efforts of women of color have driven resistance networks and liberation movements. These determined sisters have both studied history and altered it, and continue to do so today.

The American nation-states began with Europeans brutally dominating and enslaving indigenous people. The lands seized in the "New World" were worked by so-called "Indians," people whose lives did not matter to the white Europeans who, quite literally, worked the locals to death.

In his chilling portrait of the "American Holocaust," historian David E. Stannard quotes from the writings of Bartolomé de Las Casas, the Franciscan friar who accompanied Christopher Columbus on his trek to "the Indies":

Caring only for short-term material wealth that could be wrenched up from the earth, the Spanish overlords on Hispaniola removed their slaves to unfamiliar locales—"the roads to the mines were like anthills," Las Casas recalled—deprived them of food, and forced them to work until they dropped. At the mines and fields in which they labored, the Indians were herded together under the supervision of Spanish overseers, known as *mineros* in the mines and *estancieros* on the plantations, who "treated the Indians with such rigor and inhumanity that they seemed the very ministers of Hell, driving them day and night with beatings, kicks, lashes and blows and calling them no sweeter names than dogs."[1]

So savage was the violence that the Europeans waged against the people of the indigenous nations, that before a century passed, approximately 60 to 80 million Native Americans had been killed.[2]

Indian lives simply did not matter to whites who arrived on their shores; what mattered to them was getting free land and cheap labor. By 1502 the Spanish were importing shackled Africans to replace the Indian communities they had brutally decimated with abuse and disease. By 1619, the first Black laborers, known as indentured servants, arrived aboard Dutch ships at Jamestown, Virginia, an early English settlement. By 1650, the norm for Black people in the growing colonies would be a lifetime of enslavement.

For the next 200 years, Black lives mattered as little to whites as had those of the indigenous. From 1619 to the early 1800s, some 100 million people were transported in filth and chains from Africa to the Americas, with a relatively small number, nearly a million, being shipped to the plantations and fields of British North America. These dark-skinned Africans and their descendants slaved for generations in order to feed, house, serve, and enrich profit-obsessed white people. They wasted their lives to build a thriving economy that enriched their enslavers, but not themselves or their families.

These first Black Americans weren't considered enslaved workers; under British and American law, they were not even persons, but property, mere beasts of burden.

In the 1856 book *Stroud's Slave Laws: A Sketch of the Laws Relating to Slavery in the United States of America*, George M. Stroud surveys the laws governing the impoverished lives of enslaved Blacks, and portrays white America as a place of unremitting cruelty and meanness. Stroud shows how the courts of the land, North and South, served the interests of the white enslavers, but was utterly ruthless when it came to the needs of the Blacks they enslaved. Among the cases that Stroud presents to crystallize his point are *Negro Flora vs. Joseph Graisberry* and *State vs. Mann*.

In the case of *Negro Flora vs. Joseph Graisberry*, Ms.

Flora, a Black woman enslaved in Pennsylvania, attempted to use the court system to sue for her freedom. In what Stroud calls a "mockery of justice," the state's highest court ruled that slavery did not violate the state constitution even though it states: "All men are born equally free and independent, and have certain inherent and indefeasible [inexpugnable] rights, among which are those of enjoying and defending life and liberty." Stroud, a Philadelphia attorney, noted with derision that the decision was rendered by a unanimous state supreme court.[3]

In the case of the *State vs. Mann* the decision reads:

> The end [of slavery] is the profit of the master, his security, and the public safety. The subject is one doomed in his own person and his posterity to live without knowledge and without the capacity to make any thing his own, and to toil that another may reap the fruits. Such services can only be expected from one who has no will of his own; who surrenders his will in implicit obedience to that of another. The power of the master must be absolute to render the submission of the slave perfect. In the actual condition of things it must be so. There is no remedy. This discipline belongs to the state of slavery. They cannot be disunited without abrogating at once the rights of the master and absolving the slave of his subjection. It constitutes the curse of slavery to both the bond and free portions of the population; but it is inherited in the relation of master and slave.[4]

Some readers may object and ask: supreme court opinions from two states? How does that reflect the broad diversity of American legal opinion? Or: Isn't it unfair to cite to cases before the Civil War; before the 13th, 14th, and 15th Amendments to the U.S. Constitution?

While these objections have facial appeal, they do not stand scrutiny, for it remains a fact of legal life that most law is state law. Furthermore, most cases never make it to a state's supreme court.

Moreover, what changed after the U.S. Constitution was amended? In a word, little, for Southern states followed the bright, brief respite of Reconstruction with the dark night of Redemption, and proceeded, with the tacit acquiescence of the U.S. Supreme Court, to ignore the so-called "Reconstruction Amendments." This was accomplished first by attacking Black voting rights, then attacking Black voters and using state laws and state constitutions to outlaw Black voting.

If the U.S. Constitution was respected in the South, why did Reverend Martin Luther King Jr. and company have to struggle for voting rights, or even need a voting rights law? Why was the Civil Rights Movement even waged? Because across America, Black lives, as with Black votes, didn't matter.

Or did they?

During Reconstruction, Blacks were elected to state and national legislative bodies. They sat on juries and served as government officials. Perhaps more potently, Black political figures shepherded into existence free public schools and public works, and advanced women's rights. The new public schools, open to Black and white children, brought literacy to millions for whom it might otherwise not have been possible.

Of course, white reaction took the form of denigration of Black politicians, perhaps best seen in the propaganda film for white supremacy *Birth of a Nation*, which has the distinction of being the first motion picture to be shown in the White House. President Woodrow Wilson described the film as "like writing history with lightning." "My only regret," said Wilson, "is that it is all too terribly true."

The beginning of the 20th century was marked by horrific racist mob attacks on Blacks from the rural South, who in many cases were newcomers to America's major cities. Black scholar W.E.B. Du Bois called the period "Red Summer" for the sheer volume of Black blood shed.

An American Congress had indeed passed the 13th, 14th, and 15th Amendments, but they were blatantly ignored in dozens of states where the torture and terrorism of bullwhips, lynch rope, and arson were practiced with greater consistency than were the lofty promises of the amended Constitution. Yes, in theory the U.S. Constitution protected the rights of Black Americans to vote. But Southern states responded by producing a plethora of new laws to suppress Black voting, such as poll taxes, literacy tests, and grandfather clauses—laws that denied the right of voting to anyone whose grandfather hadn't voted!

Have Black votes ever mattered?

Well, they certainly have seemed important enough to suppress and steal.

The naked denial of constitutional rights for perhaps

a century lasted until the Civil Rights and Black Liberation movements demanded change.

Meanwhile, millions of Black people voted with their feet when they left the South for states in the North and West, including Pennsylvania, Illinois, Kansas, and California.

This exodus became known as the Great Migration, one of the biggest population shifts of the 20th century. Black Americans fled the ephemeral Southern comforts for the reasons people have emigrated since time immemorial: to escape the acute meanness of racial tyranny; to escape terrorist violence; to flee from economic exploitation; to seek lives of freedom and dignity; and to bless their children with hopes of better lives.

Historian James R. Grossman writes of the new period for Black life in America:

> For the first time in American history, the nation's basic industries offered production jobs to African Americans. From New York, Boston, and Philadelphia to Pittsburgh, Chicago, Detroit, and to a lesser extent, Los Angeles, factory gates opened.
>
> Work in railroad yards, steel mills, food-processing plants, garment shops, and other industries paid wages far beyond what was available in the rural or urban South. But it was more than the money that attracted black Southerners north. These jobs also represented portals into the industrial economy. These opportunities promised a new basis for claims to full citizenship—a promise

that a previous generation of black Southerners had envisioned in the possibility of landownership.[5]

For these Americans, the North was the Promised Land, and they did not see the thorns amidst the roses. They never dreamed that the new gleaming mega-cities would become traps as oppressive as the ramshackle huts and shacks they fled from back home.

They went North and West because their Black lives mattered.

But where once whites killed and terrorized from beneath a KKK hood, now they now did so openly from behind a little badge. And while it may seem like a leap to associate the historical white terrorism of the South with the impunity with which police kill in Black communities today, it is really not so great of a leap because both demonstrate a purpose of containment, repression, and the diminution of Black hope, Black aspirations, and Black life.

Indeed, the late Dr. Huey P. Newton, a cofounder of the Black Panther Party, in a 1967-era interview, likened the relations between police and Blacks in the United States as one of antagonism similar to that between the U.S. Army and the enemy population in Vietnam:

In America, Black people are treated very much as the Vietnamese people, or any other colonized people... for the brutalizing police in our community occupy our area, our community as a foreign troop occupies territory. And the police are . . . in our community not to promote our welfare, for our security or safety; they're there to contain us, to brutalize us and murder us, because their orders are to do so. And just like the soldiers in Vietnam have their orders to destroy the Vietnamese people. The police in our community couldn't possibly be there to protect our property, because we own no property. They couldn't possibly be there to see that we receive due process of law, for the simple reason that the police themselves deny us the due process of law. And so it's very apparent that they [are] only in our community, not for our security, but for the security of the business owners in the community, and only to see that the status quo is kept intact.[6]

Dr. Huey P. Newton was quite clear in revealing what mattered to police and the power structure they serve. Black lives did not matter to them in the mid-1960s, and they seem not to matter to them today. When Black men, women, and children gathered in the streets of Ferguson, Missouri, to protest the police killing of Mike Brown, they were met by a phalanx of militarized forces, armed with weapons of war. What has really changed? Did things improve under Barack Obama? How do you think things are going to go under Donald Trump?

Have Black lives ever mattered?

HATE CRIMES
June 14, 1998

The barbaric torture and murder of James Byrd Jr. by three white men—Shawn A. Berry, Lawrence Russell Brewer, and John W. King—in the tiny Texas town of Jasper has become a summertime feast for an insatiable American media, but it is a meal that consists largely of spectacle. On June 7, 1998, Berry, King, and Brewer offered Mr. Byrd a ride home. Instead, they shackled Mr. Byrd's feet to a chain and dragged him behind their truck for miles.[7]

The vigor with which the latest race murder is being covered is strikingly contrasted with the lackluster coverage of a similar case from over a year ago in Virginia, where a young Black man, in the company of a few white drinking buddies, was beaten, burned, and as he took too long to die, decapitated with an ax.

Why is one story a national firestorm, and another a local curiosity? Why is one an unquestioned hate crime, and the other merely a case of "boys being boys," or a bad mix of liquor and bad company?

This is so because the media said it was so, and because the local police told them this.

When is a hate crime a hate crime? When it is a crime of hate, or when the police say it is? And if the cops are to be the arbiters of what is, or isn't, a hate crime, who will judge the cops without bias?

In late April 1998, New Jersey state troopers pumped over 11 shots into a van occupied by four Black and Hispanic students who were on their way to basketball tryouts at Central University in North Carolina, seriously wounding three of the four young men. Thanks to the infamous "racial profiling" program of the New Jersey State Police, the four never made it to tryouts that day because they were found guilty of the unwritten crime of DWB—Driving While Black. Despite a rain of lies alleging that the basketball players were speeding, attempted to run the cops down, and so on, it soon became clear that the boys had done nothing— nothing except exist. *Ain't each of the 11 bullet holes evidence of a hate crime?*

In Chicago a man named Carl Hardiman was shot and wounded by a city cop for refusing to drop his "weapon"—a cell phone. *Ain't that a hate crime?*

New York Black Panther Shep McDaniel was brutally beaten by six cops in the Bronx as he attempted to peacefully monitor and note an altercation between police and two women. New York's finest shouted, "He's a crazy, fucking, nigger!" as they punched, kicked, stomped, and cuffed Mc-Daniel. A jury later acquitted McDaniel of resisting arrest and disorderly conduct. *Was not his beating, brutalization, trumped-up arrest and bogus prosecution a hate crime?*

On May 13, 1985, Philadelphia police dropped a bomb on a home in a residential Black neighborhood where 11 men, women, and children—members of the naturalist MOVE group—were incinerated and dismembered by cops. The sole adult survivor, Ramona Africa, was prosecuted, convicted, and sent to prison for seven years. *Ain't that a hate crime?*

In many ways, Black America remains captive to its feverish, hateful history in a land that daily mocks the claim to being "the home of the free." We have become conditioned by corporate mis-leaders who make a spectacle out of occasional acts of racial hatred, while ignoring the structural ones that degrade the everyday life of millions of Americans.

Why do we pay attention to the retail acts of anti-Black violence, while ignoring the wholesale? Far more dangerous than the white-robed KKK is the legalized malice of the black-robed judiciary. Far more destructive than the Aryan Nation are the local, armed, and uniformed police who are legal agents of an ancient, deadly hatred.

THE LAW AGAINST THE LAW
June 20, 1998

"If it took the White majority more than two hundred years to understand that slavery was wrong, and approximately one hundred years to realize that segregation was wrong (and many still don't understand), how long will it take them to perceive that American criminal justice is evil?"[8]

—Paul Butler

As long ago as 1880, the United States Supreme Court, in *Strauder v. West Virginia*, ruled that the "defendant does have the right to be tried by a jury whose members are selected pursuant to nondiscriminatory criteria." Over a century later, in 1986, the nation's highest court reiterated this principle in *Batson v. Kentucky*, for although a century had passed, it remained all too common for trials to be conducted before all-white, or predominantly white, juries, in cases where it appeared as if, besides the defendant, only the judge's robes were black. It also shows us that no matter what the Supreme Court does, the judiciary, prosecutors, and police will do what they want to with impunity, especially when Blacks are defendants. For, if *Strauder* was the "law" why did it need reiteration in *Batson*?

Strauder was ignored in U.S. courtrooms for 106 years,

just as *Batson* is today. As any law student knows, the theory of law is vastly different from its practice. Shortly after *Batson* was decided in 1986, an assistant district attorney in Philadelphia gave a class to district attorney trainees, teaching them how to violate the spirit of *Batson* by ensuring that most Blacks would be removed from jury pools. Much time has passed since *Batson*, and yet cases are upheld today where a Black defendant sees Black jurors removed for bogus reasons. What is the "law"? What the Supreme Court says, or what district attorneys do? What the cases say, or what trial judges allow?

The "law" is what is allowed every day in real cases, in real courtrooms, across America, and not what is written in dry, dusty books read by hoary scholars. Seen from this perspective, *Batson* is still not the law, despite what books may say. And if the process is not tainted enough, what of the consequences of such a process?

Recently, the governor of a state that boasts a spate of *Batson* violations—Pennsylvania—signed Senate Bill 423 into law, thereby enacting a statute that forbids a death penalty appeal based on the following:

a) claims that Blacks are more likely to be executed for the same crime than whites;
b) claims that an indigent defendant is more likely to be executed than a rich one;
c) claims that a death sentence is excessive or disproportionate to the penalty imposed in similar cases.

This is, essentially, a law against the "law." It is a proclamation of the supremacy of the political over the legal. It is a statute that explicitly enforces the value that white life matters and Black life does not. It is a law of the state that exclaims the inherent superiority of the wealthy over the poor, and that allows the basest disproportion to masquerade as "justice."

It is a statement that reflects a hellish, unequal status quo that still has not changed no matter what the U.S. Supreme Court says, and no matter how many times it says it.

It is the law of what was, what is, and what may be.

WE ARE BLIND TO EVERYTHING BUT COLOR
July 5, 1998

> "In order to get beyond racism, we must first take account of race. There is no other way."
> —Justice Harry Blackmun, *University of Calif.*
> *Regents v. Bakke* (1978)

In cases decided every day across America, the theory of color blindness said to govern the judicial process is a reflection of the flawed notion that the mere mention of race is somehow racist. Consequently, the law serves up yet another legal fiction, which obscures the complexity of real life, in furtherance of a false and fatal simplicity.

There can be no sustained study of American law without coming face to face with the racism that drenches judicial thought, in a clear, unapologetic tone that leaves no question as to the objectives of the court.

It is obvious that the objection on the part of Congress is not due to color, as color, but only to color as an evidence of a type of inferior civilization that it characterizes. Yellow and bronze, as racial colors, are the hallmarks of Asian despotisms. It was deemed that the subjects of these despotisms—with their fixed and ingrained pride for their particular culture, which accepts the subordination of the individual and community to the supreme personal authority of the sovereign, as the embodiment of the state—were not well suited to further the success of a republican form of government. Hence they were denied citizenship.

The anti-Asian bias that oozes out of the 1921 decision *Terrace v. Thompson* (U.S. District Court, Washington), for example, which is clothed in a kind of quasi-sociological justification, actually justified laws in Western regions that outlawed the sale of land or property to Japanese people, on the basis of ineligibility of citizenship. Until the 1950s, the Chinese and other Asians were denied naturalization.

Despite our pretensions of being "color blind," scholars assure us that, over a century after the Chinese Exclusion Act of 1884 became law, the court case that upheld the Act remains good law to this day.

The U.S. Supreme Court majority in *Chai Chan Ping v. U.S.* (1889), found "the presence of foreigners of a different race in this country, who will not assimilate with us" to be properly excludable. For over a century, such decisions that made whiteness the sole prerequisite for U.S. citizenship, and explicitly excluded people it deemed "nonwhite," had, at their very core, not "color blindness," but color consciousness distorted by a profound sense of white supremacy.

It is fitting here to note that in 1935, the two countries that had racial restrictions on naturalization in common were Hitler's Germany and the United States of Americas. Color blindness?

For the better part of two centuries race has been at the very heart of law in the United States. It remains so despite the latest fashion of the legal fiction of "color blindness." How people are treated in court, how they are charged, and how they are sentenced are direct reflections of what race and ethnicity they are and how such traits are regarded by white America.

Several years ago, a prominent American law professor asked his students to imagine they would wake up the next day as Black folks. The white students reasoned that such a "disability" required monetary damages of a million dollars a year for life.

Why damages, unless color *does* matter? Unless whiteness is a valued property which, when lost, demands a premium payment? And Black is devalued?

Americans are blind to everything but color.

A HISTORY OF BETRAYAL

October 29, 1998

United States history is a study in denial, for much of what is taught as history in the schools of the nations bears little relationship to the lives lived by millions of men, women, and children on the land we now call America.

Most schools teach that which is safe, and mostly false; so much so that shock and disbelief are usually the result of telling a history that reveals that many of the men called "Founding Fathers" were enslavers, visceral racists, and, in a word, creeps.

Dedicated to the erection of a "white man's republic" (as supported in the 1857 Supreme Court opinion by Chief Justice Roger B. Taney in *Dred Scott v. Sandford*), many of the nation's leaders, congressmen, and presidents were virulent racists who made every effort to deny any semblance of justice to Black freedmen in the hellish aftermath of the Civil War. How many Americans know that more than 37,000 Black men died while serving in the Union Army? The people who fought to preserve the union, who fought against secessionists and enslavers, returned to a South where virtually every promise made to them was shattered and broken, often by the very government they had fought to defend. While the war was raging, General Sherman assigned thousands of acres to freedmen, on the land that was vacated by white enslavers or confiscated. These lands, on which more than 40,000 freedmen and their families tussled with the earth to create a life, were summarily snatched away from them by the U.S. government. In October 1865, General Howard traveled to "Sherman land" to revoke titles to lands confiscated during the war, in order to return them to their previous white owners.

General Howard's instructions to the so-called freedmen? "Put aside your bitter feelings," and "become reconciled" to your old enslavers. The people who had suffered indignity and bondage for centuries, who worked to enrich the national economy, told the U.S General: "No, never," and "can't do it."

Howard Merrimon, formerly enslaved in Mississippi, described the condition of emancipated Black folk during the period of the Great Betrayal, 1865–1866:

> No land, no house, not so much as place to lay our head. . . . Despised by the world, hated by the country that gives us birth, denied of all our writs as a people, we were friends on the march. . . . brothers on the battlefield, but in the peaceful pursuits of life it seems that we are strangers.[9]

Abolitionist Wendell Phillips aptly noted that without the vote, Blacks would be doomed to a "century of serfdom."[10] He wasn't far wrong.

Blacks fought and died for the Union, and after the war they were forsaken, treated as if they were the enemy of the very nation that they had fought and bled for. Here, in the aftermath of carnage, white supremacy was the law, and Blackness was a crime. That was the reality that leads to today, the history that created the days and nights of this very hour.

When the United States was formed, it was constituted by an act of compromise that left half of the nation slave, and the other half of the nation "free." A hundred years later, and even after the raging horrors of war had ripped the nation apart, a new compromise was reached between the North and South. In the words of one supporter of President Andrew Johnson, that compromise was based on this central tenet: "Keeping the Nigger down."[11]

For a century after "Emancipation," Black folks, in the main, were denied every substantive right of the U.S. citizen: voting, holding office, jury service, freedom of travel, freedom of assembly, freedom to collective bargaining, etc.

Far from free or equal, Blacks found themselves condemned to a new life where the state took the place of the slave master, and did everything in its power to control Black labor in the interests of the landowner's class.

For most of American history, so-called "law" was merely white whim. Black life, considered cheap in slavery, became "free" and worthless in "freedom." As historian Eric Foner notes:

> Sheriffs, justices of the peace, and other local officials proved extremely reluctant to prosecute whites accused of crimes against blacks. To do so, said a Georgia sheriff, would be "unpopular" and dangerous while an Arkansas counterpart told

a [Freedman's] Bureau Agent that to take action against a planter who had defrauded freedmen "would defeat him in the coming fall election."[12]

That was the reality that leads to today. The roots of a repression that still block sunlight, and makes Black life so hellish still.

LEGALIZED POLICE VIOLENCE
March 28, 1999

"When a gang member is beaten by persons un-
known in a mixed neighborhood, and the black
gangs begin terrorizing whites, it is called racism,
a bunch of cops can ride through black neighborhoods all day beatin' ass, and call it law, when
a bunch of blacks beat one of these cops' ass it's
called mob violence."

—John Africa

A young woman, engulfed in a diabetic coma while sitting in
her car, is repeatedly shot by a corps of cops, who say they
are threatened by her. Tyesha Miller, of Riverside, California becomes a statistic.

A young man sitting in his car in North Philly is sur-
rounded by a phalanx of armed cops whose guns are pointed at him from all points. He is ordered to raise his hands.
When he does so, he is shot to death by one of the cops,
who insists he thought he saw a gun. The 18-year-old is unarmed. Dontae Dawson becomes a statistic.

An emigrant from the West African nation of Guinea
comes to America, taking an apartment in New York's Bronx
Borough. When four NYPD cops approach his door, reportedly because of a suspected rape (he was not a suspect),

he is shot at 41 times. Nineteen shots hit him. Amadou Diallo was unarmed, and will never return to West Africa.

In case after case after case, in city after city, from coast to coast, such events arise with alarming regularity, worsened by the realization that, in most cases, cops who have committed these acts, which if committed by others would constitute high crimes, will face no serious prosecution, if any prosecution at all.

They are, the corporate media assures us, "just doing their jobs," "under an awful lot of pressure," or "in fear," and therefore justified in what they do. In the language of the media, the very media that make their millions off of the punishment industry calling for the vilest sentences known to man, turn, in the twinkling of an eye, into paragons of mercy, who lament that the "fine young men" who "served their community" are in "trouble," or have "suffered enough."

The suffering of the slain, because they are young, and Black, are all but forgotten in this unholy algebra that devalues Black life while heightening the worth of the assailants because they work for the state.

The worse lie that is often trotted out when such cases occur is the term used by politicians and the media singing the praises of such people, who call them, by virtue of their jobs, "public servants." Since when have servants (of any kind) acted in the vile, arrogant, monstrous manner that many of these cops do in Black, Hispanic, and poor communities? Since when have such servants been in the position to slaughter, shoot, humiliate, and imprison the very public that they are sworn to serve?

They are servants, if at all, of the political structures of which they are a part, not of the people. They are servants, if at all, of the state. They serve the interests of capital, of the wealthy, of those who run this system from their bank vaults and corporate offices.

They do not serve the poor, the powerless, nor the un-influential.

They never have.

They are an armed force organized to protect the interests of the established, and those who own capital. The history of labor in this country is splattered by the blood of trade unionists who were beaten, shot, and crushed to the earth for striking against the trusts, combinations, and mega-corporations of capital. Who did the beating? The shooting? The crushing? The cops, who served the interests of a state that declared, as did the U.S. Supreme Court, that unions were "criminal conspiracies" and that the Constitution "was based upon the concept that the fundamental private rights of property are anterior to government and morally beyond the reach of popular majorities."[13]

Capital's voice (the media) and their agents (the politicians) unite in a chorus of support for their legalized killers, who bomb babies with impunity (remember May 13, 1985, in Philadelphia?), who shoot unarmed kids in their cars, and unarmed African emigrants, whose only capital crime is being Black in modern-day America.

This legalized violence proves that violence is not a problem for the system—when it is their own, against the people.

This awful crime must cease.

THE FOLLY OF CALLING THE FBI
April 18, 1999

"When are you Black folks gonna throw off the
KILLERS that are JAILIN' you for murder?"
—John Africa

When Black folks are beaten down by cops all around the
United States, and when they are shot down in their cars as
in the cases of Dontae Dawson of Philadelphia,[14] or Malice
Green of Detroit, or the beautiful young sister, Tyisha She-
nee Miller, who was shot more than 15 times in her car in
Riverside, California, recently—we can go on and on—one
of the first things that many Black leaders do is to announce
that they are asking for the FBI to come in to "solve" the
case. What such an announcement means, of course, is that
they recognize that local police are in no position to mean-
ingfully investigate such heinous crimes, as their interests
are in protecting "their own." But why the FBI?

Such a call sounds strange when one considers that
the FBI played a significant and openly oppressive role
in the history of African American struggles for freedom
in America, and they were deadly enemies of such leaders
as Martin Luther King Jr., Malcolm X, Marcus M. Gar-
vey, and of such groups as the Black Panther Party, RAM,
the Student Nonviolent Coordinating Committee, the

27

Republic of New Afrika, and the like. In truth, the history of the FBI shows that they have waged a secret war against Black America, and frankly, it seems counterproductive to look to them for relief from other state forces who are waging a part of their long, white supremacist war against Black folks.

James Forman, the former head of the Student Nonviolent Coordinating Committee, after being beaten by white supremacists and Klansmen while demonstrating for civil rights throughout the South, constantly requested FBI protection from the violence. Instead, they would turn up every time he was beaten, stand by, and take notes, never stopping any of the violence, but instead helping to gather dirty and derogatory personal information on civil rights workers. He finally concluded that the FBI was a part of "the governmental structure," and were, in effect, "the enemy of Black people."[15] Forman noted:

> We did not say it that way in 1963, but we did know that the FBI was a farce. It wasn't going to arrest any local racists who violated any and all laws on the statute books. Instead, it would play a game of taking notes and pictures. The files in Washington must have been growing thick even then with documents from the civil rights movements and with photographs of us all—doing everything but screwing, and maybe even that.[16]

Former FBI chief J. Edgar Hoover found it intolerable that "Negro" men would "want to be addressed as 'Mr.'"[17]

Scholar Kenneth O'Reilly writes that the job of the FBI was, in large part, to stifle Black unity:

> Division Five also worked to "prevent the rise of a 'Messiah'"—someone "who could unify, and electrify, the militant black nationalist movement." Malcolm X had been the most likely candidate, but his assassination removed that threat. Malcolm was simply "the martyr of the movement today." Muhammad was hardly a more viable threat "because of his age." In the final analysis, Division Five said, [Stokely] Carmichael and [Martin Luther] King were the only serious candidates. They both dreamed of becoming a messiah and had "the necessary charisma." Not even [William C. Sullivan, head of Domestic Intelligence] considered King to be a militant, but that was beside the point. "King could be a very real contender for this position should he abandon his supposed 'obedience' to 'white, liberal doctrines' (nonviolence) and embrace black nationalism."[18]

History has taught us that the state has its interests and the people have another; and they do not coincide.

Now, with much of the nationalist movement in pieces, some aligned with the Democratic party, some involved with community organizing, and others involved in various areas of social and cultural life, it is somewhat surreal to read of community calls for the FBI every time that a young person is murdered by cops.

Since when are they the solution? The propaganda shown by the movie *Mississippi Burning* doesn't come close to showing the true role of the FBI. It's time folks acted as if they knew that.

WHERE IS THE OUTRAGE?

1999

"Black people have begged, prayed, petitioned and demonstrated, among other things, to get the racist power structure of America to right the wrongs which have been historically perpetrated against Black people. All of these efforts have been answered by more repression, deceit, and hypocrisy. . . . City Hall turns a deaf ear to the pleas of Black people for relief from this increasing terror."

—Dr. Huey P. Newton

The much-ballyhooed recent event held in the Meadowlands, New Jersey—a benefit concert for this writer's legal funds by Rage Against the Machine, the Beastie Boys, Bad Religion, members of Chumbawamba, and Black Star—has become the food for many a newspaper or radio station, hungry for the stuff of spectacle.[19] The musicians were assaulted by a litany of complaints, and were vilified by police and their political agents, on the basis that for such musicians to dare speak out in the interest of fairness and justice for a man encaged on Death Row was some kind of violation.

Politicians raged and spluttered, and lamented that the First Amendment to the U.S. Constitution would not allow them to stop the proposed concert. Why should that so very hallowed constitutional principle hold when the players wanted to play, but be ignored when the young people and organizers wanted to pass out or sell information?

How special is the First Amendment? *It isn't.*

To the brave and principled groups that dared to play despite the bared fangs of the state's hostility, we must all send our salutes and our kudos. They have done something that was truly remarkable.

To the state, we must send our hisses, and wonder at their strange sense of Selective Outrage.

When a group of young college students were en route to Central State University and were shot by a cabal of New Jersey State Troopers after being stopped on the New Jersey Turnpike, where was the outrage?

When young men are shot by cops in the streets of Newark, Camden, Elizabeth, Asbury Park or any other city where Black people live, where is the outrage?

When there is monstrous disparity between the state's funding for students of impoverished families in Camden, and the children of wealth and means in Princeton at primary and secondary levels—where is the outrage?

When those charged "to protect and serve" fire more than 40 shots at an *unarmed man*—Guinean immigrant Amadou Diallo—while he is standing in his Bronx doorway, after which the state's propaganda forces, the white supremacist press, call for "calm" and a "wait-and-see" attitude, where is the outrage?

Given the recent attacks on Black folks and the poor around the nation, who are the unarmed victims of militarized police power and who are blown into oblivion by the police with utter impunity: where is the outrage?

If one examines these and other instances, one finds that there is no outrage, for it is not outrageous to the political and economic elite when Black and poor people are summarily executed by the state. This is exactly what is to be expected. It is nothing exceptional. It is their warped status quo.

When the system kills Blacks, there is no outrage, for it has been normalized by centuries of white enslavement, terrorism, and injustice. Such violence is simply the accepted way of how things are.

When people stand up to this system, when they unite against the morbid forces of death, the media will bay "outrage," while their real fear is the potential unity of the people, for it is in the media's commercial interest for the population to remain atomized, isolated, and divided against each other.

The unity of the people is the greatest weapon against the silence, fear, and oppression imposed by the system.

Our unity—as communities, networks, and movements—is so important. Therefore, our unity is attacked.

What makes the Meadowlands incident remarkable is that it occurred in the face of vicious, unprincipled, and naked attacks against all of those on Death Row, not just one man. Several years ago, the state and federal government cut all funding to all post-conviction legal services to all people on Pennsylvania's Death Row. They are now completely undefended, and are at the "tender mercies" of the state that wishes to kill them. That so many good people would assemble to assist the defense of just one of that number is an act of resistance to the system that would deny any meaningful defense to them *all*.

There should be outrage against a system that dares to call such a perverted system a fair one. There should be outrage against those who sit in silence when the rights of any are denied. There should be a swelling sense of outrage at the system that cries alligator tears when one man is defended, while 209 men and women remain undefended.

The death penalty is an outrage, one kept in operation by a conspiracy of state terror, a bare shadow of "defense," and the vicious political will of base prosecutors who care more for their career than what is truly just.

It is an outrage. Isn't it?

WHAT IS THE FOURTH OF JULY FOR?

June 19, 1999

"When we were the political slaves of King George, and wanted to be free, we called the maxim that: 'all men are created equal' a self-evident truth; but now when we have grown fat, and have lost all dread of being slaves ourselves, we have become so greedy to be masters that we call the same maxim 'a self-evident lie.' The Fourth of July has not quite dwindled away; it is still a great day for burning fire-crackers!"

—Abraham Lincoln

This Fourth of July, the parks, shores, and play-places of the people will be filled to the brim with tens of millions of Americans who are enjoying their vacation weekend in the hot summer sun. It is truly a holiday, and nothing else. But what does it celebrate?

We are told from our infancy that this date celebrates the blessings of freedom and liberty from oppression. While this claim is repeated year after year, the truths taught us by bitter history reveal a long legacy of oppression, repression, and death. The history of this country is rife with the foul excrescence of racialized human bondage and enslavement. Until the addition of the Thirteenth Amendment, the word "slavery" was absent from the very text of the United States Constitution. Former president, and counsel for *The Amistad*, John Quincy Adams made that point plain: "The words slave and slavery are studiously excluded from the Constitution; circumlocutions are the fig-leaves under which these parts of the body politic are decently concealed."[20]

While millions of Africans born in America were held, in the eyes of a blinded "law," as human cattle (chattel), their white enslavers were professing the "blessings of liberty" while forcing Blacks to labor in shackles and live in misery.

And now, today, more than a million African American men are still in shackles, enslaved in modern-day plantations, forced to endure conditions that are the shadows of what their not-so-distant ancestors suffered. What is liberty in the midst of these newly enslaved? Where is liberty in the prison-house of nations?

The courts, John Africa explains, are but "process houses for slavery" wherein "liberty" and "justice" are just words. Their practice is *unfreedom*, and that is the underside of the American way.

How is it that there are hundreds and thousands of new cells being built every few weeks in the land of the free? Because this is not the land of the free, but of the imprisoned and the repressed.

The revered Frederick Douglass once asked, "What, to your slave, is the 4th of July?" It was, he said, nothing but a sham. To his descendant people a century later, the same answer may be made. For, though it may be considered by most a day of rest and relaxation, the foreboding sight of a cop car in the rearview mirror is more than enough to dash such soft moments, and cases from across the country scream out the deadly risks involved in simply being Black.

In the United States today, driving while Black is a high-risk activity. For men such as Amadou Diallo, the West African in the Bronx, it wasn't necessary to drive. He was simply standing while Black. And in Black America, any of these nebulous "violations" carries an implicit death sentence.

Some may try to remember America's Founding Enslavers, if they wish: George Washington, Thomas Jefferson, et al. But it might be more fruitful and realistic to remember the names of Africans and African Americans who could not practice the simple, alleged "right" to drive securely, to walk the streets in peace, or to safely answer their doors at night: Amadou Diallo, Tyisha Miller, Abner Louima, Dontae Dawson, and on and on.

No doubt, their loving families will have somewhat subdued celebrations of America's Day of Liberty on the Fourth of July.

For millions of American citizens, that day may only bring somewhat slight respite, for too many Black families are trapped in the prison of poverty. Joblessness means, among other things, not having to worry about a holiday. What can any freedom mean when one can't afford to do anything meaningful in this commercialized pay-as-you-go society?

The Fourth of July is truly just another day.

PUBLIC SERVANTS OR PAID PREDATORS?

February 27, 2000

The trial of those charged in the slaughter of an unarmed West African man, Amadou Diallo, has ended in the predictable acquittal of his killers—four white cops.

When is a killing not a killing? Apparently, when the homicide is perpetrated by police. When police kill, it is an accident, a "mistake," an "oops!"

Let us examine how the police achieved this judicial sleight-of-hand.

As soon as the case arose, the legal forces defending the state fled the very area that the police claim to be "serving."

Why is it okay to enforce the law in a given neighborhood, yet automatically wrong to have citizens of that same neighborhood try to enforce (as jurors) some of that same law when it comes to these particular "public servants"?

In New York City in recent months, Black and Latino men have been shot for having keys, candy bars, wallets in their hands. This deadly rain of "accidents" is an official expression of Negrophobic oppression, and it can only escalate after this unholy acquittal of the four killer cops from the Bronx.

When the case began, the police immediately opted for a bench trial—before a judge, not a jury. When an African American jurist was selected, they put in a change of venue motion that put them on the first-thing-smoking to Albany, in upstate, white-bread New York. So much for the "community" that they "serve."

THE SERVICE THAT THE STATE DELIVERS IS DEATH!

What of the recent case of the young Hasidic Jew Gidone Busch, who was cornered by four cops in Borough Park, Brooklyn? Police snuffed Busch's flame by shooting him 12 times outside of his home.

Immediately, New York's mayor, Rudolf Giuliani, and Police Commissioner, Howard Safir, attacked the dead youth, and painted him as a "fanatic" whose shooting was "justified." Key to their justification was their claim that police needed lethal force to protect themselves from the Jewish man who "attacked" an officer with a hammer.

Despite the fact that eyewitnesses uniformly disputed this claim, three months after the August 1999 homicide, a grand jury exonerated all four cops and pronounced the killing "justified."

WELCOME TO THE TERRORDOME

The vile and violent attacks on Black and Puerto Rican people in the nation's capital cannot long be limited to communities of color. Consciousness does not obey the laws of geography; repression, like toxic mustard gas, seeks the lowest level.

A conservative, pro-Giuliani, Orthodox Jewish community is still, essentially, a Jewish community. And the social forces that truly run New York regard them as a minority, another flavor of difference.

Busch's life, like Diallo's life, was deemed expendable. Both men were executed twice, once at home, and then in the court system, where their lives, families, and communities were subordinated to the armed authority of the state.

According to published reports, one resident of Borough Park told a Black reporter: "Yesterday I believed that when the police would shoot down a Black man, they had a reason. Now I realize that the police can be animals—and they have the power to cover it up at all costs. The next time a Black man gets shot, I'm marching with you."

Let us hope that really happens, so that a vast movement can be built.

CINCINNATI FIRES
April 17, 2001

"The government is only as lasting as your understanding of administration. The Army is nothing without people, the Air Force is grounded without your endorsement, the ships of the Navy could never have sailed if your leaders didn't have you sail 'em, and the brutal depravity of police would be non-existent if you didn't wear the uniform."

—John Africa

After Cincinnati police shot and killed an unarmed Black teenager, Timothy Thomas, Black rage exploded in the Ohio city, igniting several nights of fire, rebellion and pain.

Like many of the race riots that rocked the nation in 1960s, the precipitating event in Cincinnati was an act of brutality and violence by police against Black folks. Police violence against Blacks has sparked indignation and rebellion from coast to coast, costing hundreds of millions of dollars in destroyed property, and hundreds of lost lives.

Much time has passed since the tumultuous 1960s, and in the intervening years we have seen the emergence of a Black political class. But we have also seen the further impoverishment of Black families in inner cities, projects, and ghettoes as communities of color have become more desolate, more isolated and more hopeless than they were in the '60s. We have seen the explosion of the prison industrial complex at rates that would've been unthinkable in the 1970s, with upwards of 2,000,000 men, women, and juveniles caged in American jails and prisons. The United States, with only 5 percent of the world's population, has 25 percent of the world's prison population!

And for too many young Black men and women, the horror of incarceration has become a perverse rite of passage, marking one's transition from youth to adulthood.

So, while things have gotten better for some African Americans since the 1960s, things have gotten demonstrably worse for millions of other, poorer, Blacks. As their economy is constantly pressured to further enrich those who are already wealthy, public schools—never quite outstanding in the first place—have gone into decline. City services have been diminished. Industries, loyal only to profit, have gone elsewhere, leaving many cities with less employment, and with the remaining jobs offering less salary and fewer benefits, while costs have gone up.

Cincinnati's riots, sparked by the police shootings of an unarmed Black teen, could have happened anywhere in America. Chronic social neglect and sense of disposability fester in cities across the country.

Instead of increased education, solidarity, and support, communities of color get increased surveillance, increased stop-and-frisks, increased traffic pull-overs, and increased militarization of police forces that target the life and liberty of people of color. In many of these cities Black people hold public office but too often function in the role of keeping the restless natives in check, keeping them suffering in silence.

The Cincinnati riots represent the eruption of youth who see clearly how the system regards them. Cincinnati is a harbinger of things to come. Cincinnati is the fire next time.

AIDING AND ABETTING
"BOMBINGHAM": THE FBI
May 28, 2001

The Civil Rights Movement of the 1950s and 1960s left several powerful images burned into the minds of millions of Americans. Those images are so deeply seared into the national consciousness that place names work as a kind of mental snapshot, better than Polaroids.

For those of a certain age in America, the mere mention of the name Birmingham evokes a dark shadow from history. It evokes the Alabama of virulent hatred, of water hoses unleashed on children, hitting with the force of a sledgehammer, of snarling police dogs biting at youngsters, of burning crosses, of firebombed churches.

The specter of Birmingham arose again recently when an elderly Ku Klux Klansman, Thomas Blanton Jr., was convicted for his role in the infamous terrorist bombing of the 16th Street Baptist Church there in 1963, where four little Black girls—Denise McNair, Addie Mae Collins, Carole Robertson, and Cynthia Wesley—were murdered, and others were maimed and wounded.

While the media and government have praised the prosecution of Blanton, the real question is, why did it take so long?

It took so long because of the Federal Bureau of Investigation—the FBI.

In American myth the FBI of Hoover's day was projected as the best of the best. Its members were squeaky-clean grown-up versions of the boy scouts. The movie *Mississippi Burning* paints them as true blue heroes, knights of the realm who work for freedom, justice, and vanilla ice cream.

In truth, the FBI played a pivotal role in the Civil Rights Movement, but not the one reflected in the movies.

For the better part of 40 years, the FBI held secret tapes—which were finally released for his recent trial— Blanton and other KKK members confessing to bombings and other acts of violence. The FBI also had a deep-cover informant in the KKK (Gary Thomas Rowe) who participated in a number of bombings and other violent crimes for which he was never prosecuted.

The FBI was too busy, it seems, investigating, harassing, framing and "neutralizing" Black leaders such as Martin Luther King (Jr. and Sr.!) and Malcolm X, and groups like the NAACP, CORE, SNCC, the Black Muslims, the SCLC, the Mississippi Freedom Democratic Party, and a host of others.

If you still have any illusions about the role of the FBI during that historic period, consider the observations of American scholar Howard Zinn, who was teaching at the time at the historically Black Spelman College in Atlanta. Several of his students were active in the movement, and Zinn often showed his solidarity by accompanying them at demonstrations. When SNCC members Chico Neblett and Avery Williams went to the county courthouse to feed and assist those trying to register to vote, they were beaten, knocked to the ground, assaulted with cattle prods, and jailed by local police. Across from the courthouse was the federal building. That federal building, writes Zinn,

> also housed the local FBI. Two FBI agents were out on the street taking notes. Two representatives of the Justice Department's Civil Rights Division were also there. We were all watching the arrest of two men for standing on federal property urging people to register to vote. I turned to one of the Justice Department lawyers.
>
> "Don't you think federal law has just been violated?," I asked.
>
> The Justice man said, "Yes, I suppose so."
>
> "Are you going to do something about that?"
>
> "Washington is not interested."[21]

Washington was also not interested in the four little girls who were dressed in their Sunday best when they were blown to bits in their community church. Washington's inaction protected the racist white terrorists, not the lives, security, and dignity of the Black children, their families, and the congregation.

For to do otherwise would be to violate the status quo regarding the nation's racial caste system and its relation to state power. The FBI's secret tapes evidencing Blanton's role in the terrorist attacks are real-life *X-files*.

OF COPS AND COURTS
March 2, 2002

Several of the cops convicted in connection with the vicious, brutal, terrorist assault of Abner Louima in a Brooklyn police precinct have been graciously granted their freedom by a U.S. appeals court. Citing insufficient evidence and the ineffectiveness of trial counsel, the state's highest federal tribunal reversed the convictions of Charles Schwartz, Thomas Bruder, and Thomas Wiese, on conspiracy and civil rights charges.

The assault of Abner Louima, as many are aware, was a crime of unmitigated savagery, when police wrongfully arrested him, a young Black man, outside a nightclub, and rushed him, manacled, to a police station in Brooklyn, where they rammed a broomstick into his rectum, then took the bloody, feces-covered stick, and forced it down his throat, shattering his teeth along the way.

No one heard his screams?

No one saw his attackers beat, pummel, or brutalize him?

No one? Not one cop, in a place swarming with cops? Far be it from this writer to suggest that the cops should somehow have lesser constitutional rights than the average Joe. The point is, however, that they have considerably more.

That such heinous acts of sadistic violence took place

at all in modern-day America speaks volumes, and not just about the sense of impunity with which police conduct themselves. That such acts happened in an official government building—a city police station—and no one, to this date, has ever come forward as a witness, also speaks volumes about a society that tolerates its police perpetrating such acts.

When cops get busted, they often do so only after a grand jury has charged them (average folks have a bill of information filed against them).

When they do go to trial, they are represented by the best legal talent that money can buy, often paid by their local labor lodge (average folks must scrape the money together to pay for a lawyer, or accept the services of a public defender).

If they are convicted—which is exceedingly rare—it is usually on lesser offenses (for more rarely still are they charged with the more serious crimes), and if sentenced, they often get moderate terms, unlike average folks, who are deluged with charges and receive heavy sentences. And even in the unlikely event that they are harshly sentenced, there is a profusion of cases involving prosecution of cops who have stolen, lied on the stand, been corrupt or brutal, and yet have had their sentences cut by judges who are not otherwise known for leniency or compassion.

From the barbaric brutes of the Los Angeles Police Department to the thieves of the infamous 39th District in Philadelphia, to those who aided or abetted the sick and depraved terrorist attack on a Black Haitian in Brooklyn's police precinct, judges have been openly solicitous of state authority's every right, for, truth be told, they are ever brothers, under the robe/uniform, who look out for each other.

"WE HAVE NO COUNTRY"

October 19, 2002

Time marks the minds of us all.

Every people has its traumas and dates that trigger memories and nightmares. In Panama, for example, mentioning December 20 evokes the dwellings of the poor, laid to waste by the airplanes and land forces of the United States, which staged an invasion of Panama in order to secure perpetual dominance over the Panama Canal, for which the barrios of El Chorrillo were pounded into powder and ash, and thousands were left homeless.[22]

For people in the United States, all you need to do is mention "September 11," and no more is required.

The mind races to images of fire, dread, death, and devastation as traumatic as any endured by survivors of military invasion.

Yet September 11 also evokes other memories for other people, for it marks a date when Africans in a hostile America rose up against the misery imposed by their white enslavers, and fought back for the bright light of freedom. It was dawn, September 11, 1851, when a group of slave-catchers converged on a farmhouse in a little town called Christiana, in Pennsylvania's southeast corner. Present were the enslaver, Edward Gorsuch, his son, Dickinson, a U.S. marshal named Henry Kline, and several other armed white men. They

49

thought they were out on just another day's work—the work of enslaving—but they met five Black men and their wives, who had no intention of giving up their freedom. Gorsuch made his demand, telling the now-free Blacks, "You had better give up," and adding, "for I have come a long way this morning, and want my breakfast; for my property I will have, or I'll breakfast in hell."

William Parker, who had escaped to freedom some 12 years before, had no intention of turning over anybody, and called down to Gorsuch, "See here, old man. You can come up but you can't go down again." Black historian Ella Forbes recounts the events in her stirring work *But We Have No Country: The 1851 Christiana Pennsylvania Resistance.*

As the posse attempted to enter his house, Parker "met them at the landing; and asked, 'Who are you?' The leader, Kline, replied, 'I am the United States Marshal.' I told him to take another step, and I would break his neck. He again said, 'I am the United States Marshal.' I told him I did not care for him nor the United States. At that he turned and went down stairs."[23]

Parker's position, in light of the passage and extension of the Fugitive Slave Act, which threatened all Black people, whether fugitive or free, with seizure and a passage into bondage, was simple. He said, "The laws for personal protection are not made for us, and we are not bound to obey them. . . . [Whites] have a country and may obey the laws. But we have no country."[24]

One of the Black men in the farmhouse began to weaken, a man named Pinckney, who said, "We'd better give up."

His wife, Hannah, picked up a machete (called a "corn cutter") and grimly announced she would cut the head off of the first one who tried to surrender.

For a time, Parker and Gorsuch argued over slavery, and each quoted the Bible to support their views, but each knew that words would not decide the argument. Parker's wife, Eliza, seeing the necessity of reinforcements, blew her horn to summon members of the Black neighborhood militia. As she sounded her horn the Marshal shot at her with a pistol, but missed. As scores of militiamen appeared, the U.S. marshal withdrew, but the stubborn Gorsuch and his men remained. The elder said, "I'll have my property or die in the attempt." He tried. He died. When Dickinson tried, he was shot and wounded.

As night fell, Parker and two other Black men took to the Underground Railroad, en route North. United States President Millard Fillmore, who signed the 1850 Fugitive Slave Act into law, dispatched 45 Marines to Christiana, and they arrested scores of people. Thirty-six local Black men and five white Quakers were later tried for treason. The men, defended by the abolitionist congressman Thaddeus Stevens, were acquitted by a jury in 15 minutes!

Parker, meanwhile, like thousands of other Blacks, made way for Canada, after stopping off at the Rochester, New York, home of the great Black abolitionist Frederick Douglass. Historians have considered the Christiana Resistance the first shots fired in the looming Civil War. Philip S. Foner has called it a "major harbinger" of that war.

Christiana proved that the fight for freedom in America

would be a fight not merely with words, not merely on paper, but with blood.

For millions of Americans of that day, September 11 meant a day that could not, and would not, be forgotten.

THE OTHER CENTRAL PARK RAPES
2002

"The ideological space for the proliferation of this racialized fear of crime has been opened by the transformation in international politics created by the fall of the European socialist countries. Communism is no longer the quintessential enemy against which the nation images its identity. This space is now inhabited by ideological constructions of crime, drugs, immigration and welfare. Of course the enemy within is far more dangerous than the enemy without. And a Black enemy within is the most dangerous of all."

—Angela Y. Davis

There was, without doubt, a wild and horrific crime committed against a young woman in the green depths of New York City's Central Park, in the cool nights of 1989. But she was not the only person against whom a crime was committed. Five boys—Yusef Salaam, Kharey Wise, Kevin Richardson, Raymond Santana, and Antron McCay—were each victimized by a judicial system that saw them in the same shallow racist terms that the media were portraying them. Like most poor folks, the boys were hustled into court and provided with defense counsel that was barely more than a presence.

In the days following the Central Park rape, as well as during the trial, Donald J. Trump took out full-page ads in city papers viciously lamenting that these "animals could not receive the death penalty." The boys were duly bum-rushed to one of New York State's prison hell-holes, where they were tarred with one of the worst of all tags: "rapist." In prison culture there are few epithets that are more deadly, with perhaps only "baby raper" being worse. These five youngsters endured years of such horrific conditions, some of them for over a decade.

And when the time came for an elusive false freedom, they faced another hell in a city where their names had become anathema. For as they suffered, so too did their families. The boys' mothers recently wrote to the head district attorney and said: "We have suffered for thirteen years but it seems like an eternity, while the so-called justice system refused to hear our laments, or even objectively review our many legal concerns regarding the many improprieties that we perceived to be evident in this case. It has been our hope although not our belief that we would be treated fairly and democratically given the confession of Matias Reyes and the forensic verification validating his admissions."

The mothers of the Central Park Five have endured the unendurable as their boys were swallowed up into the gulag and emerged with permanent scars upon their very souls. One wonders what would have happened if Mr. Reyes had not come forward.

In a word, *nothing*.

One has to wonder how many other Americans are rushed through a voracious, greedy, and soulless system, to languish in the joint under processes that are virtually identical to those endured by Yusef Salaam, Kharey Wise, Kevin Richardson, Raymond Santana, and Antron McCay.

What is most striking about the Central Park Five is their ordinariness; they are anybody's son, in any city, at any time. Their fate is not unique.

And so the Central Park jogger rape case folds, and it now seems that those boys got raped, by judges, by defense lawyers, by prosecutors, by juries, and by "the white nationalist media," to quote Black novelist Ishmael Reed. The very media that sensationalized and demonized the boys 13 years ago, and sold ad space to call for their deaths, now make new millions off their exoneration.

Many ask what went wrong. The question really should be, what is the difference between this case and hundreds—if not thousands—of others? What *is* the difference? The answer is, not much. It happens every day in a nation where the lives of Black, brown, and Latino families don't matter.

WHEN A CHILD IS KILLED
February 22, 2003

There is something unutterably terrible about the death of a child.

The universe seems to pitch and turn, and fall into itself when something so unnatural occurs as a child leaving the realm of the living. On Christmas Eve 2002, it happened.

Indeed, more than that happened.

A 12-year-old boy was shot into eternity on that date, shot by a cop who would later claim that the boy was running—with his hands in his pockets—from a car suspected to be stolen. Putting aside, for a moment, the absurdity of the image of a child running with his hands in his pockets, the state police would later claim that they used lethal force and killed Michael Ellerbe because a police officer had fallen down, and it was thought that he had been shot.

The city of Uniontown, Pennsylvania, is a fair-size town, roughly 150,000 people, located in Fayette County in the southwestern part of the state. The percentage of Black people in Uniontown is roughly equal to the percentage of Blacks in the nation's population as a whole, but population, standing alone, means little if the people who comprise it have neither representation nor power.

There was a coroner's inquest into the killing, but it empaneled an all-white jury. Despite the eyewitness testimony of a young white boy who saw the shooting from his window, the jury and the judge running the show declined to charge the cops with anything. The witness recalled that he saw the two troopers shooting at the boy. A few days later, the local district attorney would announce that she would not charge them with anything.

In the wintry weather of February, some 300 Uniontowners and others gathered at the Fayette County Courthouse to protest the tragic killing and to demand justice.

Michael Hickenbottom, the boy's father, spoke simply and eloquently to the gathering: "I'd like to thank particularly God, who blessed each and everyone of us to be here today. The Pennsylvania State Police shot and killed my son, and now they're trying to cover it up. I know there's love in this world when I look out and see all of you here today."[25]

The family has filed a federal lawsuit charging civil rights violations and wrongful death.

Some of the marchers expressed anger that nationally known Black leaders did not join them in their protests against the Fayette County criminal "justice" system. Many of the big names were invited, but none showed.

Pictures of the child show a boy with a sweet half-smile, a knowing glint in his eye, and a sense of the immortality that all children seem to delude themselves with.

Once again, the police have set forth the "Amadou Diallo defense," the "I thought my partner was hit" bit. They are allowed the old "I-was-just-doing-my-job" excuse, and are thus able to, quite literally, get away with murdering children.

A child is dead, shot in the back by a minion of the State.

A Black child is dead, a hole burrowed into his heart.
Once again, a boy does not live to become a teenager.
A child is gone.
And, according to the Law, no one is to be charged for it.
A Black child is dead . . . again.

TRYING TO SURVIVE TO 90 WHILE BLACK?
December 2, 2006

It's boy's night out, and a group of brothers is holding a bachelor's party at a neighborhood club. One of them is particularly thrilled, because his marriage to the woman he loves is just hours away.

But he will never marry, because a pack of wild undercover cops will execute him, with a deadly onslaught of 50 bullets fired at him and his friends.

The crime? Cruising while Black. Sean Bell, unarmed, died single at 23.

And the spectacle media explain it away saying it may have been a case of "contagious" shooting—one cop fires, two cops fire, then three cops. Get the picture?

It's a kind of social illness, like alcoholism.

But neither Sean Bell, Trent Benefield, nor Joseph Guzman was armed. According to some reports, one of them *said* he was armed.

Like the madmen who launched a preemptive war on the unsubstantiated claim of weapons of mass destruction, undercover cops launched an urban preemptive war on unarmed young Black men, reportedly based on unsubstantiated suspicions. *Fifty shots fired*. Homicide, and serious injury.

No cell phones, no wallets, no candy bars to mistake for a threat, for such trifles are no longer deemed necessary.

In America, Blackness is sufficient threat to warrant that whites use lethal force.

Even maleness isn't required, as shown by the recent shooting of an elderly woman who allegedly allowed a drug dealer to use her home. Katherine Johnston, having lived almost 90 years, was shot to death while trying to defend her Atlanta home after it was attacked by undercover cops.

According to a neighborhood snitch, he never claimed her house was a drug site, despite police pressure to do so.

No significant quantities of drugs were found at the home.

What was *her* crime? Trying to survive to 90 while Black?

What's more dangerous—drugs, or armed undercover cops kicking in doors looking for bad guys?

Police suspicion, it seems, is a weapon of urban war. Several years ago, writer Kristian Williams noted a case in which a whole community was held under siege because of police suspicion. In his remarkable 2003 book, *Enemies in Blue: Police and Power in America*, Williams recounted an amazing story:

> The racial politics of police suspicion are well illustrated by the North Carolina State Bureau of Investigation's "Operation Ready-Rock." In November 1990, forty-five state cops, including canine units and the paramilitary Special Response Team, lay siege to the 100 block of Graham Street, in a black neighborhood of Chapel Hill. Searching for crack cocaine, the cops sealed off the streets,

patrolled with dogs, and ransacked a neighborhood pool hall. In terms of crime control, the mission was a flop. Although nearly 100 people were detained and searched, only 13 were arrested, and one of them convicted. Nevertheless, and despite a successful class action lawsuit, the cops defended their performance and no officers were disciplined. When applying for a warrant to search every person and vehicle on the block, the police had assured the judge, "there are no 'innocent' people at this place. . . . Only drug sellers and drug buyers are on the described premises." But once the clamp-down was underway, they became more discriminating: Blacks were detained and searched, sometimes at gunpoint, while whites were permitted to leave the cordoned area.[26]

How many of the armed employees of the state who shot Johnston, Bell, Guzman, or Benefield will ever feel their wrists manacled together, see the inside of a cell, or experience the despair of Death Row?

We *know* the answer, because we've seen this movie before. Paid leave—which amounts to paid vacations—a whitewash of an investigation, and a "they-were-doing-their-jobs" are all that ever happens.

It's a damned shame.

DEATH IN A CELL

January 12, 2009

The strangulation death of 19-year-old Ronnie L. White in a jail cell in Upper Marlboro, Prince George's County, Maryland, after 36 hours of confinement has confounded Ron Harris, the teenager's father.

Mr. Harris recently told reporters, "It's been six months, and still nobody can tell me who killed my son or what happened leading up to his death." Harris added, "I want to know why there is still so much secrecy in this case and why, after all this time, I still don't have answers."

And despite the empanelment of a county grand jury looking into the case, the Harris family still has no answers, for the grand jury disbanded without bringing any indictments.

Community groups, from the People's Coalition for Police Accountability, the advocacy group CASA de Maryland, and the Princes George's County chapter of the NAACP have protested the death of Ronnie L. White, braving the bitter December winds to gather together to demand a true, fair, and impartial investigation into his death, and the prosecution of all involved.

That's because White died 36 hours after his arrest in connection with the death of a Prince George's county cop, who was hit by a car allegedly driven by White.

After the events of June 2008, White's father is left with little more than questions. "My son died in solitary confinement in a jail," Mr. Harris said. "They knew who was working in the unit and where he was that day. The doors were locked, and only a few people had keys. Yet, after all this time, they say they don't have enough evidence to know who did it? Why not?"

OSCAR GRANT AND YOU

January 17, 2009

Like you, I've seen the searing cell phone footage of the killing of 22-year-old Oscar Grant, of Oakland, California.

And although it's truly a horrific thing to see, it's almost exceeded by something just as disturbing: how commercial media have responded in defense of the police who killed him.

This defense, that the killer cop who murdered Grant somehow mistook his loaded gun for his Taser, has been offered by both local and national news reporters—even though they haven't heard word one from Johannes Mehserle, the Bay Area Rapid Transit cop who wasn't interviewed for weeks after shooting and killing an unarmed man.

If you've ever wondered about the role of the media, let this be a lesson to you. You can see here that the claim that corporate media are objective is but a cruel illusion.

Imagine this: if the roles were reversed, that is, if bystanders had footage of Oscar Grant shooting Officer Mehserle, would the media be suggesting a defense for him?

Would Grant have been free to roam, to leave the state a week later?

Would he have made bail?

The shooting of Oscar Grant III is but the latest, West Coast version of Amadou Diallo, of Sean Bell, and of hundreds of other Black men. And as with them, don't be surprised if there is an acquittal, again.

Oscar Grant is you—and you are him—because you know in the pit of your stomach that it could've been you, and the same thing could've happened.

You know this.

And what's worse is this: you pay for this every time you pay taxes, and you endorse this every time you vote for politicians who sell out in a heartbeat.

You pay for your killers to kill you, in the name of a bogus, twisted law, and then pay for the State that defends them.

Something is terribly wrong here, and it's the system itself.

Until the system is changed, nothing is changed; we'll just be out in the streets again chanting a different name.

THE ARREST OF HARVARD SCHOLAR DR. HENRY LOUIS GATES

July 30, 2009

If the arrest, humiliation, and resultant brouhaha over Harvard scholar Dr. Henry Louis Gates has taught us anything, it is that people in the United States still dwell in separate worlds, ones that rarely meet.

And while some wags have rushed to tell us that the incident reveals little more than the continuous clash of class, I beg to differ.

If anything, it shows us just the opposite. When it comes to Black people of whatever wealth, status, class, or prominence, the usual rules don't apply.

Indeed, handling Blacks seems to always require exceptions to standards that apply to most everyone else.

Consider this: most Americans can agree with the familiar aphorism that "a man's home is his castle."

Not Black men.

How else could "Skip" Gates get busted on his doorstep for disturbing a nonexistent peace?

In law, homeowners' property rights do not end at their front door. They extend all the way to the street, ending at the curb. This is an appurtenance.

Imagine if a person slips and falls on the sidewalk in

front of a home. That person has a claim on the homeowner, not the city.

Dr. Henry Louis Gates was busted not because he violated the law, but because he violated the emotions of the cop—Sergeant James Crowley—who entered his house. The policeman was angered when Dr. Gates initially refused to exit his house, and it angered him further when Professor Gates demanded that the public servant provide his identification.

President Barack Obama was right when he called the policeman's arrest of Dr. Gates "stupid," but, as usual, politics prevailed when rednecks responded with howls of protest. One need look no further than the email sent by Boston police officer and National Guardsman Justin Barrett, in which Officer Barrett descends to hate speech to refer to Dr. Gates as a "banana-eating jungle monkey." "At the time, Boston Police Commissioner Edward F. Davis vowed that there would be a termination hearing in seven to 10 days," reported the *Boston Globe*.[27] "But four months later, Officer Justin Barrett, who was accused of writing an e-mail that called Harvard professor Henry Louis Gates Jr. . . . remains on administrative leave and is still collecting his $70,500 salary."[28]

Cops get paid vacation for their hate speech and bigotry. What do their victims get?

Will a beer at the White House put this fire out?

I doubt it, for it ignores what happens every day, in dozens of states, to countless men and women who don't have Harvard Ph.D.s, or friends in high places.

The sad truth is, being Black in America is akin to being born low-caste in India, where separate and unequal rules remain, despite promises in their constitution.

Barack Obama's presidency hasn't changed reality, but may mask it, by providing cover for the ugly things that Blacks endure in a nation where white elites claim a false "post-racialism."

A "beer summit" on the lawn of the White House won't change that either.[29]

WHEN A GRAND JURY FINDS BEATINGS
TO BE "HELPFUL"

August 13, 2009

As the contretemps surrounding Dr. Henry Louis Gates and the Cambridge Police Department falls out of the news cycle to become fodder for late-night comedians, we learn, if anything, that even a president has limits when it comes to "teachable moments."

For, as any schoolteacher could have taught him, learning is a two-way street. When the student is closed to the lesson, ain't nothing getting in. (And America ain't trying to hear nothing about its racist present!)

Dr. Henry Louis Gates, a man possessed of a healthy sense of humor, has even joked about the incident publicly, and in my imagination, I can even hear his distinctive chortle as he answers the questions, "Are you all right?" with the quip, "Yeah—I'm okay; the only thing hurting is my dignity."

Precisely because of his renown and status, Dr. Gates, a prolific writer, acclaimed academic, and PBS broadcaster, was spared the violent indignity meted out against most Blacks who rouse the anger of white cops in this country.

Most African Americans are not so privileged, as shown by the beating administered to Nadra Foster, a KPFA radio producer who, in August 2008, was attacked, kicked in the head, and handcuffed, by at least eight cops.

Because Ms. Foster lacks the level of national prominence of Dr. Gates, Nadra's story did not make it to the evening news; nor did the Black presidential candidate at the time announce he was a "friend" of this Black mother, who worked for over a decade at the Pacifica station as a volunteer producer, nor that her beating, kicking, handcuffing, and arrest were handled "stupidly," as, of course, they were.

That's because, in America, what happened to Ms. Foster ain't anything new.

Just recently, a Philadelphia grand jury, expertly led by a local district attorney, refused to indict half a dozen cops who brutally beat, kicked, bludgeoned, and stomped three young Black men who were allegedly suspects in a local shooting. (The three were later acquitted.) The grand jury refused to return indictments despite videotapes from a hovering helicopter showing the men struck repeatedly by more than a dozen cops as they lay face down in the street.

To add insult to injury, the grand jury report (scripted by prosecutors) insisted that the beatings were "helpful" rather than "harmful." I don't think the initial Rodney King grand jury, which cleared members of the Los Angeles Police Department, even went *that* far.

But news is "man bites dog," not the status quo, but the unusual. And Black people, men, women, and children, being beaten by cops isn't unusual—*even if on tape*.

There'll be no frosty mugs of beer waiting on the White House patio for the three young men beaten and battered in Philadelphia streets; nor will there be national coverage for a Black mom brutalized by a platoon of police at her community radio station.

The violence committed by police against such folks, it seems, doesn't offer "teachable moments."

WHEN RACISTS RULE POLICY

September 13, 2009

Imagine being Van Jones: a young Black man from a poor family, a graduate of one of the best law schools in America (Yale), who uses his gifts and energies not to make a buck for some soulless hedge fund, but to make a difference in his neighborhood of Oakland, California, by organizing the community around creating better jobs, stabilizing the environment, increasing clean energy, halting police violence, and improving education.

Imagine what such a man must've felt to see an unprecedented presidential campaign by another young Black man, who, from modest economic means, also graduates from one of the best law schools in America (Harvard), and spurns lucrative offers from rich law firms to become a low-paid community organizer on Chicago's west side, the city's poorest and Blackest neighborhood.

Van Jones must've felt that Barack Obama was a man after his own heart: a man who came from the poor and returned to the poor, to serve and organize amongst them. He must've also thought that this was the coming of a new age, a new era of profound social change in America.

So Van Jones takes a post as the Obama administration's green energy czar, a field he's passionate about. His mission will be to provide green jobs in Black communities, and to conserve natural resources as part of a larger shift away from America's addiction to oil.

But, almost immediately, Jones comes under attack from forces in America that really don't want change.

Egged on by "conservative" shout-show hosts, Jones was being labeled "racist," and that old Cold War charge that should've died with the fall of the Soviet Union, "communist."

Such neoconservative trantrums should've had little impact on a president who has been called "racist" and "socialist," by the same people. These are the ideological descendants of those who spat on Black children trying to go to schools during desegregation, people who called Martin Luther King Jr. a "communist" so loudly that he was under FBI surveillance to the day he died.

For these Americans, change means fear. In their dark imaginations, the only people who want change are communists.

It shouldn't have had an effect, but it did. Van Jones resigned to protect the Black president who wouldn't protect him.

It reminded me of Lani Guinier, another brilliant, Yale-trained Black lawyer, who got left hanging when racists dubbed her a "quota queen" when she was nominated for a post in the Clinton administration's Justice Department.

If racists can ostensibly lose an election and still dictate policy, then, have they really lost?

It seems to me that the loudest voices screaming "racist" are the most racist, who stand for a status quo that only serves themselves.

THE DEATH PENALTY DERIVES
FROM LYNCH LAW

March 10, 2010

The Anti-Death Penalty Movement is an offshoot of the international Human Rights Movement, that was originally advanced by non-profit organizations and grassroots groups, and later, by a variety of sovereign governments.

It is noteworthy, then, for us to cite the successful abolition of the death penalty in Kenya, in 2009.

We should also note the fact that the rate of American juries meting out death sentences has fallen to its lowest level in 30 years.

And finally, several months ago, the group that was perhaps most instrumental in fashioning the death penalty in the United States, the American Law Institute, announced it would no longer participate in formulating laws governing use of homicide for purposes of punishment. The Institute, a distinguished group of 4,000 judges, law professors, and lawyers, was the group that initially proposed the aggravating and mitigating circumstances that the U.S. Supreme Court adopted in 1976 when it reinstated the death penalty.

And yet, despite this, the death penalty is alive and well in the United States. Why?

It makes no sense ethically or economically, but most politicians seem to be wedded to it.

That's because at its core, the death penalty derives from, and thus replaces, lynch law.

Is it mere coincidence that the states that execute people most frequently are Southern ones? This is also generally true when we examine the establishment and expansion of the American prison system. After the Civil War, when law forbade whites to continue to enslave Blacks, states in the former Confederacy established the convict leasing system, by which states leased out the labor of prisoners to private parties. In his superb book *Slavery by Another Name: The Re-Enslavement of Black Americans from the Civil War to World War II*, Douglas A. Blackmon writes that during this period "whites realized that the combination of trumped-up legal charges and forced labor as punishment created both a desirable business proposition and an incredibly effective tool for intimidating rank-and-file emancipated African Americans and doing away with their most effective leaders."[30] Instead of being a financial burden, leasing incarcerated Blacks to businesses was a way local governments actually turned a profit.

In essence, these states made a private institution a public one—and both Black men and women became "slaves of the state."

The U.S. death penalty system performs a similar function. It has socialized, or made public, that which had been heretofore the province of individuals: lynchings.

LIFE IN DARK FLESH IS NOT EQUAL
TO LIFE IN WHITE FLESH
July 10, 2010

The manslaughter verdict returned against former Bay Area Rapid Transit cop Johannes Mehserle for the videotaped murder of Oscar Grant sent hundreds of protesters back into the hot streets of Oakland, California, Grant's hometown.

The corporate media scratched their collective head, essentially asking: "Why protest when the guy was convicted?"

The protesters know, however, that the court system bent heaven and earth to return the lightest verdict possible—involuntary manslaughter—and that Mehserle likely faces probation instead of four years in prison, the maximum he could possibly receive. After all is said and done, Mehserle may end up doing less time that rapper Lil Wayne did for only possessing a gun, rather than lethally using one.

Protesters know that Mehserle got a non-Black jury, hundreds of miles from Oakland.

They know that any of them could have been Oscar Grant, unarmed, shot to death on tape, and the same thing would have happened.

Of course, the corporate media don't get it.

If Oscar Grant were the aggressor, and charged with a killing, would he have been able to freely leave the state the way Officer Mehserle fled to Nevada days after killing Mr. Grant? Would he have been able to transfer his trial

hundreds of miles away? Would he have been able to select an all-Black jury—or one from which all whites were
purged?

If the killing were videotaped, would he too have been
convicted of the lesser crime of involuntary manslaughter?

Everyone who honestly considers these questions
knows the answers. What does this say about the health of
our society and our justice system?

It says, quite loudly, that there's one law for some, another law for others.

It says that life in dark flesh is not equal to life in white
flesh—and those who take to the streets of Oakland and other cities across the nation know this in their hearts, minds,
and blood.

GERONIMO

June 4, 2011

On Thursday, June 2, 2011, came word that former Black Panther leader Geronimo Ji-Jaga (né Elmer G. Pratt) died in exile in Tanzania.

Geronimo's life was one of intense and almost total warfare, from battles in his youth as a soldier for the U.S. Empire in the steaming jungles of Vietnam, to his membership and leadership of the L.A. chapter of the Black Panther Party, where he fought for his people.

The FBI-inspired killing of L.A. Black Panther leader Alprentice "Bunchy" Carter led to Geronimo's rise as the chapter's deputy Minister of Defense, and during a police raid on the Central Avenue office on December 8, 1969, Geronimo so prepared the site that it withstood over six hours of a police paramilitary assault with automatic weapons and grenades.

Geronimo's prominence and shine in the shadows of Hollywood so disturbed the state, local, and federal governments that they framed him for a murder that it was impossible for him to have committed, and sent him to prison for 27 years.

When Geronimo was freed, it was because of an insistent, national movement, and because federal government files revealed he was nearly 300 miles away when the murder took place, and because the state's chief witness was not only an LAPD undercover agent, but a snitch for the L.A. district attorney's office as well as the L.A. Sheriff's Department, an agency that formerly employed him.

Upon his liberation, Geronimo toured the country to thank his supporters, then left the land of his birth to join a small expatriate community near Dar es Salaam, Tanzania.

Like several other ex-Panthers, he could never again trust his life nor his freedom to the U.S. government.

And though he spent the balance of his years under a brilliant African sun, one suspects he longed for the rhythms of his native Louisiana, which remained in his speech and its accents.

It was in Louisiana, after all, that he learned about Black armed self-defense, for this was fertile ground for the Deacons for Defense, an armed organization that resisted and forcefully countered Ku Klux Klan terrorism in the region.

Geronimo Ji-Jaga, a warrior for his people, has returned to his ancestors.

WHILE RAGE BUBBLES IN BLACK HEARTS
August 20, 2011

It has taken a while to reach this conclusion, but upon reflection, it is inescapable.

Why, after over a half century of Black voting, and the election of more Black political leaders than at any time since Reconstruction, are the lives, fortunes, prospects, and hopes of Black people so grim?

Our education system is in shambles, with a drop-out rate nearing 50 percent in most central cities; Black communities are either ignored or gentrified into oblivion; joblessness stalks families by the highest percentage since such figures were first recorded; and Black families face foreclosure (and its concomitant result—homelessness) at rates far exceeding those for any other demographic: a direct result of the mortgage scams that lined the pockets of Wall Street banking executives and their minions.

In cities boasting Black mayors and Black police chiefs, police violence against citizens continues unabated, and the prison-industrial complex traps generations in chains.

One is forced to conclude that Black America suffers maladies similar to those faced by continental African nations: a segregated neocolonial system in which a political class gives the appearance of freedom and independence while perpetuating racial oppression and financial exploitation.

Sadly, electing more Black politicians does not equal more Black political power. For, in this surfeit of Black representation, voices of discontent are muted, while rage bubbles in Black hearts and minds.

And rather than Black politicians speaking for those who voted for them, they too are muted, more loyal to party than people—more anxious to not rock the boat, even when water rushes through the breached hull.

They speak to them, preaching patience, while home burns. And they mimic white politicians, echoing their words, while "representing" communities that could not be more desperate.

If Black politicians are to do the very same thing as their white colleagues, why have them at all?

What's the difference?

Neocolonialism at home and abroad.

TROY DAVIS: MOVEMENT LESSONS

September 9, 2011

The state murder of Troy Davis of Georgia demonstrates both the limits and the successes of the Anti–Death Penalty Movement.

It may seem inappropriate to speak of successes when an innocent man is poisoned to death by judicial decree, but though they were partial, there were successes nonetheless.

Organizing the support of people like former U.S. president Jimmy Carter, Pope Benedict XVI, bishop Desmond Tutu, and former FBI director William Sessions was no small feat. It shows the power and diversity of solidarity with a movement that reaches across lines of color, faith, nationality, and political station.

The movement's success was also fueled by revelations of people like Antoine Williams, who was one of the state's trial witnesses. Williams later stated: "After the officers talked to me, they gave me a statement and told me to sign it. I signed it. I did not read it because I cannot read. I felt pressured to point at him."

Was there police coercion in the Davis case? The district attorney certainly thought so, as shown by his remark: "Oh, well, they were probably coerced by the defense too, so that balances it out, and we should still kill him."

Think about that.

What power of coercion does the defense possess? Handcuffs? Threats? Criminal charges? Jail cells? Death sentences?

That any prosecutor can say something so dopey and maintain influence is, well, nuts.

The movement organized in solidarity with Troy Davis amassed, remarkably, close to a million signature on petitions.

But signatures on paper or online do not send quite the same message as do people in the streets.

If, perhaps, a million people had marched, Troy Davis might still be alive today.

It is bitterly ironic that William Jefferson Clinton—America's so-called first Black president—got laws on the books to prevent serious judicial review and remedy. He did this, of course, by supporting and signing into law the notorious Anti-Terrorist and Effective Death Penalty Act—a law that forced federal judges to defer to state courts on criminal law and limits death-row appeals.

Troy Davis's family and supporters have brought much to the Anti-Death Penalty Movement. I hope their indignation with the system further advances their mission, purpose, and struggle.

In so doing, they insure that Troy Davis will never be forgotten.

WHAT DO YOU CALL A JUDGE
WHO MAKES RACIST STATEMENTS?
March 4, 2012

A United States federal judge, one of the most respected and powerful actors in the nation's entire judicial system, sends a joke to a close circle of friends.

So far, so good.

But the joke is a racist insult against both the sitting President of the United States *and* his mother.

The word gets out, and the judge promptly apologizes and insists he isn't a racist.

Of course he isn't.

A judge, someone sworn to protect the legal, civil, and constitutional rights of all U.S. citizens, privately distributes racist jokes about the President of the United States: but he's not a racist.

Indeed, if the media are any measure, the only people portrayed as racists these days are Black people: like Minister Louis Farrakhan or the late Dr. Khalid Abdul Muhammad.

A few years ago, I saw a man standing in a Ku Klux Klan robe announce on a nationally televised talk show that he *wasn't* a racist.

When no one is racist, then racism becomes invisible.

It becomes the province of "hyper-sensitive" Blacks, who are called racist when they point out racism.

And, meanwhile, beyond symbolism, lies a reality as bitter and as repressive as ever before—for millions.

Question: What do you call a judge who makes racist statements?

Answer: "Your Honor."

THE TRAYVON MARTIN CASE

April 12, 2012

News of the Trayvon Martin case has rushed around the globe at cyber speed, due in large part to social media.

It had all the markings of a national tragedy, and of course, is an ongoing one, despite recent charges.

But what seems most overlooked in all the news and reporting is an understanding of what has historically come before.

Florida has a long and nasty history of events such as these, but often the antagonist is a cop, not a civilian playing cop, as is the case here.

In May 1980, Miami's Liberty City erupted into an orgy of flame, rage, and righteous indignation, stemming from the police beating of 33-year-old Arthur McDuffie, a Black insurance executive.

McDuffie wasn't just beaten—he was *beaten to death*—by four police officers. An all-white jury later acquitted all four of *all* charges.

My memory of Mr. McDuffie could've been substituted by a slew of other names, most long forgotten by all but family or friends, casualties of a long and dirty war waged by white supremacists.

People like 21-year-old Randy Heath, killed in Hialeah,

Florida, by a cop who was later acquitted. And Timothey DeWayne Thomas—anybody remember his name?

Anybody?

Nineteen years old, and slain while moving through his own neighborhood of Over-the-Rhine, in Cincinnati, Ohio.

His killer? A white cop, who, though later indicted, walked free after being acquitted.

Indeed, when the Philadelphia Police Department dropped a bomb on a residential neighborhood home, killing 11 Black children, women, and men and incinerating two city blocks that destroyed the homes of 250 people, there were no acquittals, for there were no charges.[31] No charges in a massacre.

Yes, there were distinctions, but they are distinctions without a difference.

For all these cases speak to the cheapness of Black life in the eyes of a U.S. justice system that permits white cops to beat, shoot, bomb, maim, and kill with impunity.

In the Trayvon Martin case, we have a guy playing cop, and a dead 17-year-old Black boy.

Close enough.

FOR RODNEY KING THE STRUGGLE
IS FINALLY OVER
June 17, 2012

Mention the name Rodney King, and people react.

They might react in different ways, but they react. For almost no one is neutral.

His name is evocative because it ties you to one of the biggest urban rebellions in U.S. history.

The 1992 Los Angeles riots followed the acquittal of a phalanx of cops who beat King brutally, an act that was documented on videotape!

When a predominantly white jury in Simi Valley acquitted the cops, L.A. streets exploded in rage.

It was the proverbial straw that broke the camel's back.

Not since the 1960s have we seen riots so intense or so destructive.

The riots made Rodney King famous, or infamous, depending on one's perspective.

The image of Mr. King, his face battered, asking plaintively, "Can we all get along?" has entered the realm of history, and with it a question we have yet to answer truthfully.

Rodney King, age 47, was found dead early Sunday morning at the bottom of his pool, apparently drowned.

For Rodney King, finally, the struggle is over.

TRAYVON AND THE WAR AGAINST US
June 19, 2012

For a brief moment in time, the name and fate of Trayvon Martin broke through the daily media fog and touched the lives of tens of thousands of people, motivating them, mobilizing them, and moving them to take direct action against the gross inaction of the state.

Youth across Florida walked out of high schools and took to the streets. People in dozens of cities marched, seemingly spontaneously, against a racial caste system that seems to consider people of color to be guilty until proven innocent.

Many of these young Americans took their anger to the streets because they sensed an unsaid truth: it could've been them.

It could've been them.

And these protests take place amidst the greatest institutional violence against Blacks since the height of the Civil Rights Movement. By that, I mean the silent assault of mass incarceration, or what law professor, Michelle Alexander terms "the New Jim Crow."

And it matters not that Trayvon's killer wasn't a cop, as is usually the case. He was an informal auxiliary to a system that polices Black life, and holds our every act under suspicion.

The South, for centuries, was an armed white army in which every white male was empowered by law and custom to control Black life, by any means necessary.

Trayvon was judged guilty of walking while Black and breathing while Black, as are many, many Black and Latino youth every day.

No matter what the result of the Trayvon Martin case—I happen to think that acquittal is down the line—the New Jim Crow pecks at Black, Brown, and poor lives daily, destroying any future they may've once dreamed of having.

What we learn from Trayvon's case is that organizing makes a difference, protest has impact; for without the pressure of protest, there would be no counterforce against bigotry in American society.

That lesson must translate to a call for resistance against the vast social injustice of the prison industrial complex.

When more Black men are in chains today than at the dawn of the Civil War—when enslaving people was legal—or when the South African system of apartheid was in full swing, mass protests are a necessity.

TEARS OF SORROW AND RAGE

November 2, 2012

For decades, the Oakland Police Department has been the focus of fear.

Fear because the agency, which years ago recruited heavily from the South, had people on staff that used their office to exercise their hatred of Blacks through social repression and violence.

For a brief time, the Black Panther Party put a crimp in their strut, as it became a local, and then national, force of resistance to police departments' repeated assaults on Blacks.

But the Black Panther Party is no more, and the repression has come surging back.

Adam and Jeralynn Blueford knows this dark reality all too well, for on May 6, 2012, their 18-year-old son Alan was shot and killed by the Oakland Police Department's Miguel Masso.

Alan was one of countless youngsters forced to submit to the department's outrageous stop-and-frisk tactics. Alan, rightly, was afraid of such contact, and following his instincts, took flight.

Miguel Masso chased him and killed him.

Now Alan's parents are demanding answers, but all they're getting in response are lies.

The story of what happened has changed at least half a dozen times, and Oakland's political officials have promised much, and delivered nothing.

For, forced to support either those who voted for them or the Oakland Police Department, Oakland's politicians invariably opt for the latter. Thus, from the people that are sworn to represent them, the people get evasion, or worse, silence.

For the Oakland Police Department has money and power; and when have you seen *any* politicians turn their backs on either?

As for the members of the family of the teenager whom they will never hug again, they continue to organize resistance to the menace of state violence, impunity, and repression.

THE DORNER DILEMMA
February 18, 2013

The short but utterly fascinating police career of Christopher Jordan Dorner has captured the attention of millions. Dorner, a fired Los Angeles cop, vowed war against his former colleagues and almost made good on his threats. Citing the police department's institutional racism and an unfair disciplinary proceeding that resulted in his termination of employment, the ex-cop pledged to exact revenge and unleashed a deadly rain of bullets on several of his fellow officers.

Trained as a sniper in the agency's elite squads, Dorner sent shock waves of terror through the highest ranks of the agency by targeting the families of officers. For 10 days he struck and moved, leaving the urban landscape for mountainous territory nearby. After a series of shootings, he escaped to an abandoned cabin, where more than 100 cops eventually converged to permanently "retire" the former cop.

Using pyrotechnic tear gas, they launched a grenade into the cabin, covered the doors, and waited for the raging fire to do its work. The blaze raged for hours, the last weapon deployed in Christopher Dorner's war.

Many are left pondering the forces that triggered Dorner. Fired after a questionable internal hearing, this Black cop turned on the very forces that had trained and nurtured him. He was called a "monster" and worse by reporters, pundits, and police. If true, he was a monster of the LAPD's making.

What did he see?

What did he experience that turned his heart to ice?

We may never know. But we await the next Dorner—angry, embittered, soured on the job—and determined to deliver his own "burn notice."

THE DORNER MANIFESTO

February 26, 2013

In the news business, yesterday's news is, well, no longer news. It's stale, old, useless. Yet this rush for what's new often ignores that which bears closer scrutiny. I speak of the memorandum written by LAPD's former elite officer Christopher Jordan Dorner, who went on a homicidal rampage and was later killed during an armed conflict in the hills of Southern California.

This document, titled "Last Resort," runs some 10 pages long, and news accounts have not given it a full or fair portrayal. Many, perhaps most, reporters opined that he was obviously crazy, thereby suggesting that his own stated basis for his anti-LAPD actions were unworthy of consideration. These are the journalists who perform their services and serve the powerful, not the public.

One well-known journalist all but bragged that he received a package from Dorner, yet didn't read its contents. Instead, he dutifully turned it over to police.

Amazing.

I don't have Internet access, but someone had the kindness to send me a hard copy of Dorner's text. What I read was, to say the least, stunning. If you want to see behind the so-called "thin blue line," I urge you to read it. It really is a remarkable first-person account of Christopher Jordan

Dorner's life in the LAPD, and his treatment there, including his vigorous responses when someone used a racial epithet in his presence.

In one example, he cites the free use of the word "nigger" by a cop in his vehicle. He told the fellow officer that it was unacceptable, but the cop just kept using it. Dorner stopped the car, grabbed the offender, and choked him. When the incident was reported, only one other cop admitted that they heard the hateful language. But I again urge you—read Dorner's text for yourself. It will not only give you insight into the inner workings of the LAPD, more important, it will give you insight into the media.

Dorner repeatedly implored journalists to investigate his claims. But there's little chance now. It's old news.

A HARSH LIGHT ON NEW YORK'S CRIMINAL JUSTICE SYSTEM

April 8, 2013

The riveting documentary *Central Park Five* was an explosive example of what scholar Michelle Alexander has termed "the New Jim Crow," but upon reflection we find that it wasn't so "new" after all.

Five young Black and Latino boys, charged with raping a white woman, were sacrificed on the unholy altar of political expediency and blind ambition, cut up, ripped from their lives and families, and thrown into the hellish furnace of prison, for years, to burn and weep despite their innocence.

Documentarian Ken Burns and his daughter Sarah Burns have produced a work that shines a harsh light on New York's criminal justice system, where all of its elements, police, prosecutors, defense lawyers, and the press, failed to heed the most fundamental feature of fair trials—the presumption of innocence—and they therefore became agents, aiders, and abettors of acute injustice.

But, while the Burns's work is brilliant and indeed heart-breaking in its recitation of the crimes committed against the five boys, one feature seems to be missing.

There is no discussion of the judiciary, especially the appellate courts. We know that the trial judge slept while this travesty shattered the young boys' lives, but were any appeals filed?

Any post-conviction writs? Any federal proceedings?

It is possible that none were filed, given how bleak many of the families felt after the 1989 trial and convictions.

But if they *were filed, that story too must be told, for if so, it would* show the rank corruption and the political servility of appellate courts, which failed to do justice for five children—and in so doing, damned themselves, as well.

WILL TRAYVON MARTIN'S KILLER BE ACQUITTED?

July 8, 2013

By the time these words reach you, perhaps it will all be over.

"It" is the Zimmerman trial in Florida.

I have no idea how the trial may have boosted ratings for CNN, or CNBC, for that matter, but I'd bet it helped increase the usual low summer viewership.

In this place—a prison population—every man with a mouth wants to discuss the case: In the chow hall. On the walkways. In the gym. On the yard.

Not even the buxom beauties of *Love and Hip Hop* have garnered that much attention.

"Are you watching the trial?"

"Who do you think is gonna win?"

Questions bounce like basketballs, as all eyes are locked on this, the latest "trial of the century."

The trial of George Zimmerman for killing unarmed 17-year-old Trayvon Martin has snatched a level of public attention that hasn't been seen since the O.J. Simpson murder trial in the mid-1990s.

I believe, frankly, that Zimmerman will be acquitted.

I may be wrong, but I don't think so.

I've never seen a defense lawyer utilize, so skillfully, the jiu-jitsu-style techniques of witness flipping.

In all honesty, the state's prosecution witnesses became defense witnesses.

And where the defense was adroit, the prosecutor bumbled and fumbled.

I may be wrong—I *hope* I'm wrong—but I don't think I am.

THE VERDICT: BLACK LIFE IS AS CHEAP AS DAY-OLD PRETZELS

July 14, 2013

It may have started with a bang, but it ended with a whimper.

The acquittal of George Zimmerman for the slaying of 17-year-old Trayvon Martin was, for a generation of youth, a wake-up call.

Young people around the country made this their cause, and believed, as only young people can, that justice would prevail.

But belief and knowledge are two very different things. While it is true that national protests forced the state of Florida to try Zimmerman, they did not result in the ends they sought.

Mr. Zimmerman, the son of a judge, and defended by a lawyer who is the husband of a judge, received a trial, but not one that most folks have ever seen.

An almost all-white jury threw it out after roughly a day and a half of deliberations.

What does it mean? Well, it means precisely what you think it means: Black life is as cheap as day-old pretzels.

It means that white life is privileged, and important. It also means that white fear is the operative perspective from which all court action flows.

For, if we reverse the two principals here and Trayvon had survived this encounter, who can doubt that he would be en route to Starke, Florida, the home of Death Row and its infamous death chamber?

Trayvon would've had an overworked and underpaid public defender, one who would've considered a life sentence a victory.

As long as this holds true, then talk of equality is just as fantastic as stories of Santa Claus.

What we talk about freedom, justice, equality, and fair trials, it is just that: talk.

When one enters the courtroom, the talk ceases.

It's time for legal war.

TRAYVON IS ONE, THEY ARE MANY

July 21, 2013

The Trayvon Martin case is rightly the straw that broke the camel's back, for it shows, with unusual clarity, how Black life is so easily trivialized.

But it is not alone in this endeavor.

The way the corporate media have responded to this tragedy is its own form of trivialization; a feeding frenzy of sheer spectacle, the exploitation of emotion, and endless, directionless discussion, leading less to light than to commercials.

For the media offer the episodic, while they ignore the systematic.

Thus, Trayvon's case attracts the lights and videos, but the many others who fall, especially to police violence, draw little interest.

Absent from most discussions is the targeting of a system that cages more people than any other in history. Lost from the orgy of spectacle are the hidden faces of mass incarceration that impacts millions.

For attention to the episodic elicits tears, while contemplation on the systematic brings the challenge of change.

If "Stand Your Ground" gets repealed, it does not change the system that treats many youths as expendable.

Several months ago, by just one vote, the U.S. Supreme

Court condemned the practice of sentencing juveniles to life in prison without the possibility of parole.

Of all the jurisdictions in America—indeed, in the whole, wide world—Pennsylvania ranked first in life incarcerations of juveniles. *First.*

But juveniles aren't only the targets of the prison industry, they also face shuttered schools, rampant joblessness, and the fear and loathing of their elders.

They face tomorrows of emptiness.

They face the faceless fury of a system that damns them to half-lives at their birth.

Trayvon is one, they are many.

TRAYVON WHO?

August 8, 2013

If the media are any measure of the mood of the masses, then the sound and fury of the Trayvon Martin case is over.

In place of the rage of protest there is now silence, and "the Beast"—the media—moves on in search of new prey. A missing white female? A windfall from the state lottery? An Obama-Putin dust-up?

Cool.

The rage of millions now gets submerged under the dark, roiling waters of yesterday, to bubble briefly and drown in the muck and mire of memory.

As for "leaders," both civil and political, aside from their lame efforts to repeal laws, they have no idea how to attack the real problem, and they return to their primary jobs to keep the masses cool, to tamp down their furious anger, and to keep a false peace.

And things just get worse and worse.

National civil rights groups, tied at the hip to the Democratic Party, work in tandem to keep the many cool, lest true resistance arises.

The late, great scholar-activist Manning Marable, in his 2002 work, *The Great Wells of Democracy*, noted how local activists, often at odds with national groups, pushed for change, and used imagination, insight, and grassroots power to build movements against the racist violence used by police against Black people.

Wrote Marable: "Such struggles bring into the public arena diverse and sometimes contradictory ideological and social forces. In the Cincinnati grassroots resistance movement, a wealth of new ideas were brought out in public brainstorming sessions, especially in the areas of public policy issues and economic development."[32]

Marable concludes, "virtually unnoticed at the local level, in hundreds of black communities across the nation, successful models of resistance are flourishing."

Trayvon Martin's life and sacrifice are too precious to be left in the hands of politicians.

People must "organize, organize, organize," to quote the late revolutionary Kwame Ture, to build resistance movements to protect and defend Black life.

It must begin, as all life begins, at the grassroots.

THE OUTRAGEOUS AMERICAN NORM
December 18, 2013

An Indian diplomat, Dr. Devyani Khobragede, charged with filing false employment records for her housekeeper, is arrested, hauled into a U.S. Marshal's office, strip-searched, and subsequently released.

In India, the event raises quite a ruckus, and Indian nationals express outrage, amid calls for diplomatic retaliation against the Americans.

In reminds us of the imprisonment and perp walk of French politician (and former International Monetary Fund bigwig) Dominique Strauss-Kahn after he was named a suspect in a rape of a Senegalese hotel employee, Nafissatou Diallo, some years ago.

Both cases rest upon what has been normal, standard operating procedure in American police practices: the humiliation of the accused.

In modern-day America, such police practice is largely aimed at Black and Brown people; those who have long been the subject of public humiliation. So much so, that such treatment has long been normalized; it's just the way things are done here in "the land of the free."

When foreigners experience the treatment that Americans of color endure every day, they are shocked.

The question is, *why aren't we?*

The reason seems simple. America's repressive, punitive, and humiliating system is supported by media and by the political classes, for such treatment is usually reserved for those already deprived of full social status: Blacks, the poor, and immigrants.

For them, every day is humiliation, especially as the rich and the super-rich accrue more and more power, and more and more impunity to ethics and law.

Several months ago, the U.S. Supreme Court ruled that strip searches were proper even for something as minor as a traffic stop.

When a system becomes so flush with power, it can only further consolidate as it expands, impacting more and more people.

Why should any of us be surprised?

THE LAST DAYS OF PRESIDENT OBAMA
February 13, 2014

One day soon, the administration of President Barack Hussein Obama will come to an end and enter the realm of U.S. history. Eight years will have passed, true, but it will pass with a swiftness that is difficult to articulate. Barack Obama, son of a Kenyan goat herder, and unsuccessful civil servant, will yield his place to another. And while history will have certainly been made—the stuff of books, museums, and presidential trivia—another kind of history, a quieter kind, will also have been made.

Written more in song than on paper, the history of Black Americans—those whose lives do not seem to matter—will record not the best of times, but far too often, the worst of times. Unemployment, dropout rates, foreclosures, mass incarceration levels will show significant gains, and paradoxically, the deteriorating state of the national Black community. Eight years will have passed, and by every measure Black life will have become more precarious, more challenging, more raucous, and more brutal. Some will say that the concerns of Black America shouldn't be his, for he is president of all America. But before all others, Black Americans have been his most loyal constituency. Of all constituencies, why should those who are the most supportive get the least of everything else? What kind of political representation is that? Moreover, what other constituency would tolerate such treatment?

Africans in America have had a long and tortured history of loyalty to institutions that do not reciprocate their support. Colonial governments, political parties, the Army, state governments, and yes, presidents. Yes, even a Black one. Symbols are powerful things, but when they are empty of substance, they become hollow—like now. You'd think that perhaps Black lives might begin to matter more under the leadership of a Black president. But have they?

SNAPSHOT OF BLACK AMERICA
February 16, 2014

The trial of a middle-aged man for shooting and killing a 17-year-old Black boy after hot words over so-called "thug music" that resulted in a hung jury instead of a murder conviction, shows us that all is not well in America.

The lives of Black males seem to matter least in the United States. This has been the case historically, and remains true today.

This fact has such staying power because to white America—and far too often, to Black America as well—Black lives just don't matter much.

Some will undoubtedly dispute this, but what might have happened if it were an older Black man getting into a scuffle with white teenagers about their loud music? Imagine a Black man getting annoyed at heavy metal cranking out of a car full of white teens. Imagine the white kids telling off the Black guy when he attempts to have them lower the volume on their music, and when things escalate, the man unloads into the vehicle, killing one of the white teenagers.

Can anyone doubt that the Black shooter is going to get a one-way ticket to Florida's Death Row?

This thought experiment offers a sad commentary on the law, on the courts, and on society at large. It is also a dim reflection on how Black men are still perceived in America.

White people fear Black men. It may be deep and irrational, but that doesn't make it any less real.

In fact, it makes it more so.

A century ago, during the teens of the 20th century, Blacks—men and women—just a generation out of slavery, experienced a national wave of brutal, white racist mob violence.

Blacks were lynched by the thousands in what scholar/ activist W.E.B. Du Bois called Red Summer.

This violence went on with the silent acquiescence of governments, state and federal. In fact, in many cases, state officials assisted and cheered on the crimes.

One of the triggers of the violence? Whites' anxiety that Black men, newly freed, would seek white women as sexual partners.

That psychology of fear continues today, now shielded by the illusions of politics, law, and entertainment.

A black teenager mouths off to a middle-aged white guy, and the man doesn't see a boy, a teenager—he sees a Black, and fear and rage floods his neurons.

That's a snapshot of Black America 2014.

It ain't pretty, but it is what it is.

TRAYVON'S AMERICA

March 24, 2014

A youngster goes out for a snack, simply something to munch on, and a sweet drink to wash it down with.

A man nearby sees him, and "suspicion" arises.

In a matter of moments, the unarmed teenager is dead, and the shooter calmly claims self-defense.

The cops come, summoned by a passerby who witnessed the deadly encounter. They chat with the shooter, perhaps exchange information in the way usually done at a traffic accident, put in a call to the coroner, and leave.

Imagine the dialogue:

"Hey, guys, it's self- defense."

"Yeah—looks like self-defense to me!"

"Yeah—it looks like a good shoot."

"Yup, the kid punched me!"

"Hey, no biggie: self-defense. Good shoot. You have a good night!"

No arrest. No real investigation.

Case closed for weeks.

Now, imagine the same events, but with a slight change of place. The shooter is an older, bigger Black man.

The teenager is a white rap fan, who wears a hoodie. He's unarmed. And he's lying face down in the street.

How do you think the cops would've responded then?

The fact is, you *know* how they would've responded. And it wouldn't have taken weeks, it would've taken minutes.

Who can doubt this?

And what does this say about our system, our society, and each and every American who is a pixel in the picture?

Trayvon Martin is just the name you now know. There are many nameless, faceless Trayvons.

And the real tragedy is, there will be more.

The system isn't broken.

It's rotten.

WILD IN THE STREETS

May 25, 2014

Imagine that a group of armed men run into a business, rob it of $100,000 and change, sexually assault a woman, and even steal food from them, before vanishing.

What would you call them?

What would the news media call them?

Some years ago, in Philadelphia, young people would rush into stores downtown, enter in large numbers, and rip off clothes and sneakers, fleeing amid mass confusion. The media called them "flash mobs," and public commentary denounced them as "animals," "savages," and "criminals."

Politicians rushed the mic to condemn them and promised swift and terrible retribution for such "unacceptable" acts. When some of the kids got arrested some time later, judges spat sentences of contempt and time at them.

Remember the first group?

They were city cops. Narcs.

They hit local bodegas, and cut wires to security cameras before robbing Latin American business owners.

What were they called by politicians, prosecutors, and the press?

"Officers."

These events happened several years ago. After years of "investigations," guess what happened?

Not much.

Sure, a few of the perpetrators—cops—got fired. But no charges were filed. And in the absence of charges, some, perhaps all, will get their jobs back—with back pay.

No harm done. "There's nothin' to see here, Keep it movin'."

In New York some names ring like bells: Ramarley Graham, Amadou Diallo, Sean Bell . . . injustice after injustice after injustice.

And politicians—especially Black politicians—are as silent as church mice.

This is not random. Nor is it mere happenstance.

This is institutional. This is systemic.

And this goes deeper than we know.

Over a generation ago, when police bombed the home of MOVE members in Philadelphia, they set a precedent. It was a precedent of impunity, a crystal clear example of state terrorism.

The violence and the impunity has spread like cancer, and it impacts every Black and Brown community in the country.

And when people were silent about the carnage deployed by police against the Black families in the MOVE neighborhood, they subtly gave the green light for such violence to openly continue. The wave of violent repression that has rippled out since, one which has no precedent in American history, continues to drown out the lives of Black families and communities.

We must unite to build a movement to end police violence—and the prison-industrial complex that criminalizes communities of color—once and for all!

POLICE IN THE AGE OF SOCIAL MEDIA
July 7, 2014

The scenes are, unfortunately, all too familiar.

A person is beaten, ruthlessly, relentlessly, by a cop (or group of cops).

A video is released, and, at least initially, public sympathy flows to the beaten figure on the bottom.

Before long, however, the official narrative takes hold: the beaten was belligerent, combative, resisted arrest, or, worst of all, was on drugs!

That's all that's needed for the story to go away. Done!

In California, a 51-year-old grandmother is pummeled by a cop who beats her with a flurry of punches. He hits her like she's a man in his prime.

In occupied Palestine, 15-year-old Tariq Abu Khdeir is seen punched, kicked, and stomped by cops in black uniforms, who cart him away in a waiting vehicle.

The grandmother? Police say she was playing in traffic.

The teenager? Cops said he was with boys who had knives.

So they beat them.

The videos are chilling. They are Rodney King, without the batons. They are Delbert Africa, without the rifle butts.

And they are SOP—standard operating procedure.

It's what all too many cops do.

Until people began seeing actual footage of police in action, the police and the media were able to play down reports of beatings and abuse.

But now that we find ourselves in the age of social media, we become witnesses to the intolerable fact that police beat who they want, and shoot who they want, simply because they can.

A COP SHOT 18-YEAR-OLD
MICHAEL BROWN EIGHT TIMES

August 11, 2014

Once again, an unarmed Black youth has been killed by a cop.

And while the facts surrounding the shooting are presently unclear, what *is* clear is that a cop shot 18-year-old Michael Brown eight times.

According to at least one eyewitness, police killed Brown as he stood with his hands up in the air.

To anyone familiar with American history, this is not a rarity.

Such atrocities occur as a result of a systematic function of police across the country to track, target, and repress the nation's Black population.

That has been the case for generations.

And as indignation and outrage arise in Black hearts in response to outrageous treatment, we see voices trotted out to call for calm. Never do those calling for calm become voices calling for true justice, for justice is equality—and who dares demand that cops be treated like the people that they oppress, or that the oppressed be treated with the same dignity and respect as everyone else?

Americans of color seems to have no influence over the repressive forces, and in fact, no political office in America does. They have been bought off, paid off, or both.

Listen to the voices of politicians of any color.

Listen to the raging silence.

Needed in the suburbs of St. Louis, Missouri—and in every Black community in America—are independent and uncompromising Black revolutionary collectives—determined to protect the lives and well-being of Black people, period.

Existing political structures, silent in the face of perpetual violence, have failed us, and cannot be made to serve our interests.

It's time to learn from this, and build for our future necessities.

1, 2, 3 FERGUSONS

August 17, 2014

For over a week, the media, and millions of viewers and readers, have been focused on the ever-changing events of Ferguson, Missouri, where a local teenager, Michael Brown, was shot to death by a white cop.

What has been consistent and unchanging is the level of outrage among Ferguson's Black residents—men, women, and young people who have resisted every attempt to silence or sidetrack their efforts.

Their efforts?

To achieve the arrest, prosecution, and conviction of the white cop—Officer Darren Wilson—who shot and killed Mike Brown.

Their efforts are fueled by indignation, fury, and a long train of police repression.

They haven't let anything—ot promises, provocations, politicians, or police—turn them away from their objective.

The system has used weapons of war—sniper rifles, armored personnel carriers, submachine guns and other implements of military violence—to intimidate the people, to threaten the people, and to silence the people.

They only continued their marches demanding justice for the killing of Michael Brown.

They faced sweet-talking politicians promising peace;

police with dark faces promising protection; preachers praying for placidity; and they kept on marching.

They were threatened with arrests if they broke curfew, they received the acrid rain of tear gas, and they kept on marching.

Marching for justice for Michael Brown.

A reporter for a national cable outlet asked five teens clad in baseball hats and bright red bandanas to identify themselves.

One by one, they announced their names: Mike Brown.

They were all Mike Brown.

As they march past fear, they are indeed Mike Brown.

As are we all.

FERGUSON'S REAL "OUTSIDE AGITATORS"

August 19, 2014

As the days and nights of angry resistance rage on in Ferguson, Missouri, the corporate media embarks on its newest campaign: the proposed banning of "outside agitators."

It is ironic in the extreme to hear Black reporters, Black cops, and even Black activists launch verbal attacks against "outside agitators," for the phrase "outside agitators" was born in the minds and mouths of white Southern segregationists. It was these racists who used the term to denounce the arrival of students from the North who organized to register voters, start freedom schools, and support the Freedom Riders to break state segregation laws.

Remember Martin L. King's organization, the Southern Christian Leadership Conference? When it staged marches in Alabama, that state's governor, George Wallace, called the organization's members "professional agitators with pro-Communist affiliations."

Sound familiar? How close to "outside agitators"! The phrase begs the question: *outside of what*? The state? America?

This country is called the *United* States of America, founded upon a national Constitution. Do all citizens have the right to protest, or just some?

Is what happened to Mike Brown a local matter, or is his unjustifiable killing actually a national issue?

It's not the job of media to police protests—deciding who are "good" demonstrators, who are "bad" ones. Their job is to report what is happening, period.

Were it not for these protests, let us be frank, the mass media would've ignored the crimes police committed against Michael Brown, against his family, against his community, and against his fellow citizens—us.

If media were doing their job, reporting on the vicious violence launched against young Blacks the nation over, perhaps Michael Brown would be alive today.

Let us look at the cops, almost 98 percent of whom are outsiders to Ferguson. They work there, they kill there, but they don't live there.

They dwell in neighboring, whiter counties and towns. Who are the real outside agitators?

POST-FERGUSON

August 25, 2014

As the body of Michael Brown is consigned to the earth, network newscasters and broadcasters are packing their gear, checking out of their hotel rooms, and setting their sights on new stories to chase.

That the tragic saga in Ferguson struck national newscasters is rare, indeed unprecedented, given the length and depth of the story.

But to reporters, stories come and stories go.

And the Ferguson story seems to be going.

Part of the reason has been the incessant media chant for the expulsion of so-called "outside agitators," seen as violence-prone troublemakers coming on the scene.

Once they were gone, tension drained away like an unwanted migraine.

But "creative tension," in the words of Dr. Martin Luther King Jr., is the very stuff that animates protests and helps fuel movements.

It is the job of the managerial class of lawyers, preachers, and politicians to reduce tensions, to de-radicalize movements, to make them manageable and compliant.

And once they become manageable, they lose their mass base and their social power. For the masses know the essential nature of the police; they see them and gauge them daily in their communities. They know they are often violent, vicious, and venal government officials. And they are hungry, anxious to oppose them.

Movements are a lot like volcanoes, which appear dormant, or sleeping.

Unseen are underground forces, churning, boiling, crashing like waves against a hidden shore.

Until one day, usually a day none had foreseen, they erupt, splashing red molten rage over miles, changing everything.

That's what movements do, and what they *are*. If hot enough, they can change everything.

Everything.

But political, media, and state forces don't want change; they want continuity, for therein lies both their profits and their power, and who wants to lose either of those things?

Thus the tragedy of Ferguson will be stuffed back into the pillow of forgetfulness.

Until next time.

THE MEANING OF FERGUSON
August 31, 2014

Before cops killed Michael Brown, who among us had ever heard of Ferguson, Missouri?

Because of what happened there, the brief but intense experience of state repression, its name will be transmitted by millions of Black mouths to millions of Black ears, and it will become a watchword for resistance, like Watts, like Newark, Harlem, and Los Angeles

But Ferguson isn't a thing from the last century—it's now.

For young Blacks from Ferguson and beyond, it offers stark and vivid lessons in contemporary political and social realities.

When Black youth dared protest the state's street murder of one of their own, the government responded with the tools and weapons of war. They assaulted free speech with gas. They attacked freedom to assemble as if Ferguson were Fallujah, Iraq.

The police acted as if they were an occupying army from another country, for that, in fact, is what they were.

And these young folks learned viscerally, face-to-face, what the White Nation thinks of them, their constitutional rights, their so-called freedoms, and their lives. They learned the wages of Black protest. Repression, repression, and more repression.

They also learned the limits of their so-called "leaders," who called for "peace" and "calm," while armored troops trained automatic weapons and sniper rifles on unarmed American men, women, and children.

Russian revolutionary leader V.I. Lenin once said, "There are decades when nothing happens; there are weeks when decades happen."

For the youth—excluded from the U.S. economy by inferior, substandard education; targeted by the malevolence of the fake drug war and mass incarceration; stopped and frisked for Walking While Black—were given front-row seats to the national security state at Ferguson after a friend was murdered by police in their streets.

Ferguson may prove a wake-up call that Black lives matter. A call for youth to build social, radical, revolutionary movements for change.

WE MUST FIGHT FOR MORE

September 21, 2014

Thanks to the corporate media, Ferguson, Missouri, has been all but forgotten.

Other sensationalist fare now fills the air with empty fluff about missing white women, snuff videos, and other mindlessness to further stoke public fear.

But to thousands of young Black people, Ferguson is as close as teeth are to the tongue.

They witnessed, with their own eyes, how young people, just like them, were treated by the armed forces of the state. The authorities' antipathy, their racist hatreds, their weapons of war pointed at the People will not soon be forgotten.

They also saw the stark emptiness of Black politicians, who, unable to resolve the crisis of the hour, uttered inanities about "body cams," proof positive that they don't really live in the same world as those they claim to represent.

Some called for "community policing," a phrase and concept as empty as the one before it, which simply means that police surveillance of Black people is more invasive than ever before, with the same violent repression.

The term is a perversion of a struggle once waged by the Black Panther Party: "community control of police."

In fact, in February 1980, Dr. Huey P. Newton, a Black

Panther co-founder, called for the establishment of a "Citizen's Peace Force," a force far different from the units we see today. Huey wrote:

> The working model for the new peace force resembles, in many ways, a citizen's militia. Conscription would mean drafting people from councilmanic districts to serve two-year terms in their own community. Young people from age 15 could serve part time, and no upward age or sex limit need be arbitrarily imposed. Basic training for draftees would reach out to ongoing schooling in various skills for those who were not returning to either jobs or school.

Dr. Huey P. Newton wrote that the Peace Force's linchpin would be "Civilian Control."

No present politician, from president to dog catcher, has come close to Huey's insights, or the progress of the Black Panther Party from the late 1970s to 1980.

None.

History lives to give us options for the future.

It lives to inspire us with visions of the possible.

A new, militant, and responsive politics must arise, energized by the young, who are clear-eyed and committed.

We must fight for more or we'll get more Fergusons, only worse.

THE TROY DAVIS TRAGEDY

October 13, 2014

If the name of Troy Davis is known to many, it is largely because of media coverage.

But the details of his epic struggle, and the denial of state and federal courts to seriously hear his claims, are much less known.

Read *I Am Troy Davis*, by Jen Marlow, Martina Davis-Correla, and Troy Anthony Davis. The book focuses on the Davis family, and reveals how the denial of justice tore the family apart.

It is a tale of misplaced vengeance, of political opportunism, judicial cowardice, and relentless struggle. It is also a tale of courage against great adversity, tragedy, and political betrayals like those of Savannah's Black district attorney, who echoed his white predecessors.

When Troy Davis was arrested on August 23, 1989, it was because he turned himself in after his sister told him about the case. He presented himself to police because he was certain that he would be cleared of any connection with the murder of a Savannah, Georgia, cop.

But the city, using coercive threats and fear, assembled an ignoble chorus of night people to sell their version of the events, and he was speedily convicted and doomed to Georgia's Death Row.

Troy's sister, Martina Davis-Correla, fought, virtually alone, to defend her younger brother's innocence, and to find qualified lawyers to take the case, for long hard years.

When a team of lawyers took the case, it was in shambles, and it took digging to find the truth: that Troy Davis was indeed innocent, and police had forced people to either testify against Troy or face charges of being accomplices to the homicide.

Nonetheless, almost all the witnesses recanted, casting serious doubt on the conviction, telling of the threats they received at the station.

A turning point came on August 17, 2009, when the U.S. Supreme Court, in a rare ruling, sent the case back to Georgia's federal court for an evidentiary hearing. At last, the evidence came in: mass recantations, including new witnesses attesting to Davis's innocence.

But none of it was enough to sway Georgia federal judge William Moore, who tossed out most of the evidence, finding recanted testimony "unworthy of belief."[33]

The ups and downs of judicial fortune raised the hopes of Troy's mother, Virginia, a deeply spiritual, prayerful woman; his sister, Martina; and the rest of the family, only to dash them against the rocks of despair.

On April 12, 2011, Virginia Davis passed away.

On September 21, 2011, Troy Anthony Davis was killed by the State of Georgia.

On December 1, 2011, Martina Davis-Correla died after a decade-long fight against cancer.

Troy Davis died from a broken judicial system.

Virginia and Martina died of broken hearts.

PLACE NAMES OF BLACK PAIN,
LOSS AND DEATH

November 24, 2014

Like a fever, the news broke, but, unlike a fever, it brought no relief.

For the news, from the perspective of the national Black community wasn't good.

The twelve-member grand jury in Ferguson, investigating the killing of a Black teenager, Michael Brown, voted for a "no true bill"—legalese for no charges against the police officer who shot and killed Brown.

Despite the fact that Brown was unarmed: no charges, no case, no trial.

The name Ferguson joins an ancient line of place names of Black pain, loss, and death. Places like Birmingham, Tulsa, Selma, St. Louis, New York, Philadelphia, and now—Ferguson.

It will have a meaning all its own.

For young people who felt compelled to hit the streets in protest of unbridled police power and legalized impunity, the challenge will be how to continue, how to fight on, and even what the fight *is*.

Some, broken-hearted, will flee this ugly episode and try to seal such a memory away.

Others will grow in radicalism, convinced that this case is the very epitome of racist injustice.

Ferguson may prove a turning point; history may one day look back on it as a flashpoint in time when the people decided that the normalization of police violence and impunity had become intolerable.

RULE OF LAW
November 26, 2014

In the ashy aftermath of Ferguson, Missouri, after more than 170 cities in the United States faced spirited and sometimes violent protests, it was disturbing in the extreme to hear President Barack Obama come out and call for respect for the "Rule of Law."

In his case, it was particularly ironic given the fact that when he was born, it was at a time when the very marriage of his white mother and Black father was still a crime in many U.S. states.

Indeed, it was only in 1967, in the *Loving v. Virginia* case, that anti-miscegenation laws—at the time the law in some 16 states—were struck down.

At the time, Obama was a six-year-old boy. In some parts of the United States, Barack Obama's very birth was considered a crime. Interracial marriage was against the law in roughly a third of the nation, and in those places, wasn't that the "rule of law"?

For law can be just or unjust.

Dr. Huey P. Newton said, "The law must serve men; not men serve the law."

John Africa, founder of the MOVE Organization, said, "Just because it's legal doesn't make it right."

In a nation that legally enslaved Africans for centuries,

one that exploited, raped, lynched and disfranchised Black folks, the rule of law means different things to different people.

We readily forget that Germany's detention and mass killing of Jews, Romani, Sinti, and Poles was legal.

Apartheid in South Africa was legal.

"Stop and frisk," until quite recently, was perfectly legal.

All were allowable under the "Rule of Law."

It took long, bitter, and sometimes violent protest to bring these injustices to light and then begin to change them.

The late Dr. Nelson Mandela was, we forget, a lawyer. But he became the head of the military wing of the African National Congress to fight against the unjust system of apartheid.

He knew, intimately, about the "Rule of Law"; that's why he fought it so relentlessly, and why he chose armed struggle.

He knew the keen limits of the "Rule of Law."

FERGUSON FALLOUT

November 30, 2014

Ferguson, Missouri has become a launch point not just for the youth of that city, but for youth across the nation.

They have stood up to automatic weapons, to hostile media, to their critical elders, and to an unresponsive federal government.

They have stood in the torrid heat, and the frozen snow.

On Black Friday they protested in more than 170 cities, advocating that Black Americans refrain from shopping, while millions mourn.

They are not all Black, yet most are youth, and their passion, joined with their will, is rewriting history.

They are unwilling to stop, for the forces they are facing are unwilling to stop.

Their splendid example is radiating around the world, touching minds and souls in Paris, in London, in Havana, in Lagos, in Rio, and beyond.

They are standing.

They are standing still.

"OPERATION RESTORE TRUST?"

December 2, 2014

The flames of Ferguson have eaten their fill, and its eerie glow has cast light on the impotence of those in the Black political class who cannot seem to solve any of the problems plaguing Black America.

Usually, when they speak, they seem to be ventriloquists who mouth the words of white politicians, drowning the deep concerns of their constituents in an ocean of empty words.

Now, a collection of prominent officials, from the U.S. president on down, have announced their intention to seriously tackle the issue of police abuse in Black communities.

Politicians, police officials, clergy, and community organizers are part of a coterie of people who have come together to restore trust between cops and the African American community.

When I saw this on TV, my head swiveled.

Restore trust?

One wonders when there ever was trust between American Blacks and cops in the first place.

The cruel and painful history of relations between police and people of color is one of predation, not trust.

Notably, Black police officers are part of this discussion, but are we to make note of the fact that, throughout many communities, over many years, they were *forbidden to arrest white people?*

Police are stationed in Black neighborhoods, but not to "serve and protect" Black people or their property.

They are there to control Black mobility, and to discipline Blacks in an attempt to minimize any threat that could be posed to white wealth and sense of security. Period.

That's the real situation, unlike the fairy-tale discussions about "restoring trust."

For what trust can exist between oppressors and those they oppress?

Nor can body cams be the great solution that their supporters suggest.

Recall that cameras caught, with crystal clarity, the brutal cop beatings of Rodney King in Los Angeles, and before him, Delbert Africa in Philadelphia.

Despite these captures on camera, both cases were thrown out; one by a jury, another by a judge.

So much for cameras, huh?

Who can trust a force that killed Black Panther leader Fred Hampton in his sleep?

Who can trust an agency that bombed Black families and their babies in 1985?

How can you restore something that never existed?

Until systems change, until cops are equally accountable to the same laws as everyone else, talk about "restoring trust" is just that: talk.

ERIC GARNER: "I CAN'T BREATHE"

December 4, 2014

The name Eric Garner is now enshrined in the grim annals of history.

It joins Mike Brown, Ramarley Graham, Alan Blueford, Dontre Hamilton, Tamir Rice, and thousands of others, who were murdered by those their taxes have helped pay: cops.

In many ways, Garner's case is even more egregious than Brown's, for it was videotaped; we see police take him down, we see police choke him, we see him struggle to live.

Now, the words "I can't breathe" have become joined with the cry, "Hands Up!"—reminders of the Garner and Brown killings at the hands of police.

Both cases are also noted for the behavior of grand juries that now appear reckless beyond belief in their inability to return indictments against cops.

The grand jury emigrated here from England, where it was called "grand assizes," a body of about a dozen knights under the direction of a baron (or some other noble), which would investigate cases and charge people.

Later, such bodies became tools of the king.

Today, they are instruments of the legal establishment, and used, just as they were under English kings, to target whom they wish, and to clear whom they wish.

Outrage stems from the long history of grand juries used to protect cops, yes, even killer cops.

The U.S. justice system is constructed to protect police, no matter how outrageous their behavior. That's just a fact.

And as the nation now celebrates historic events from the Civil Rights Movement of a half-century ago, the grim and ugly present of Black life, and Black death, in America, makes that glowing history feel hollow indeed.

POLICE TERRORISM: A NATIONAL CRISIS

December 7, 2014

The massive demonstrations rocking U.S. cities from coast to coast are loud and visible reflections of the deep anger and antipathy rising up against the long and bloody train of police terrorism in Black communities.

If you have read my writings or listened to my commentaries, you know that I describe police violence for what it is: not merely "brutality," but terrorism.

For the aim of all police violence is to instill terror in Black populations, just as was the aim of white terrorists of the past, like the Ku Klux Klan, which lynched Black men, women, and yes, even Black children.

And although the protests by young people occurring across the country are remarkable, we must remember that cop violence against African American communities ain't a new thing.

It was December 4, 1969, when cops invaded the Monroe Street apartment building of young Black Panthers, including Deputy Chairman Fred Hampton, of Chicago. There, police armed with submachine guns shot Captain Mark Clark, of Peoria, Illinois, and Deputy Chairman Fred Hampton, as he slept in his bed next to his pregnant wife. Both Mark and Fred were assassinated; at least seven other Panthers were wounded as they lay in their beds.

Not a single cop was ever charged with these murders, attempted murders, or aggravated assaults on their fellow American citizens.

Every May marks the anniversary of the MOVE massacre, when Philadelphia police dropped bombs from a helicopter, and killed 11 men, women, and children—members and relatives of the Black naturalist group MOVE.

Eleven people killed, two city blocks in Philadelphia turned to glowing red bricks and ashes, and not a single cop or city official faced charges. Only one person was sent to prison, a survivor of the bombing, Ramona Africa, who got seven years for rioting.

The movement protesting police terrorism is a remarkable thing; but it didn't begin yesterday.

Police terrorism goes back generations, and it ain't about "rotten apples" or "broken windows." It's about blocking movements for freedom, and protecting a system of racist repression.

GRAND JURY JAMMED

December 10, 2014

As demonstrations erupt in city after city in protest against the Ferguson grand jury's failure to return an indictment against a local cop there, I can't help but be amazed by the paucity of reporting or commentary on how the local district attorneys directed the grand jury regarding the laws used to determine whether a crime was committed.

Grand jurors, as a rule, aren't composed of lawyers or scholars. They are ordinary citizens.

That's why what happened there was so extraordinary.

An assistant district attorney specifically referred to, and gave jurors a copy of, a Missouri statute that indicated that police are permitted to shoot a fleeing suspect.

The problem is, that law had been declared unconstitutional by a U.S. Supreme Court decision.

Prosecutors gave the law to jurors in September. Two months later, in November, just days before the grand jury came to its decision, they corrected their instructions, but never once clearly explained that the law they had been given originally was unconstitutional.

According to MSNBC's Lawrence O'Donnell, when a grand juror asked the district attorney directly if the U.S. Supreme Court case overturned the Missouri statute, the juror was given evasive and misleading answers.

One prosecutor remarked that the grand jury wasn't a law school!

When a jury is given two instructions, one correct, and the other incorrect, it is misled, for the only result of such a practice can be confusion.

A confused grand jury is a manipulated grand jury, and the citizens of Ferguson, Missouri—and family of Mike Brown—deserve better.

Another unarmed Black person is killed by another cop who goes free.

When will Black lives matter?

DEMONSTRATING RESPECT?

December 23, 2014

Throughout much of modern American history, the seasons of mass demonstrations have been spring and summer.

Look at old black-and-white photos of the anti-war, civil rights, and Black Power demonstrations of the 1960s and 1970s, and you'll see a lot people in short-sleeve shirts and blouses.

The way folks dressed reflected the ease and warmth of the weather.

As in classic military theory, good ground conditions are crucial for waging battles.

Today, however, hundreds of thousands of people are out protesting in biting cold; in wind, rain, and even snow.

The winter protests indicate that people nationwide will not continue to accept excuses for lethal police violence against unarmed Black Americans.

Now, after the shootings of two cops in New York come calls from politicians to "suspend" demonstrations, out of respect.

The question arises, who respects whom?

When cops killed Mike Brown, Eric Garner, and Tamir Rice, who showed respect for them?

Michael Brown was literally demonized by his killer.

Eric Garner, we were told, was too overweight to

survive his choking, and should've just meekly submitted to the attack on his life.

Tamir Rice, a child, was "big for his age," and "scared" cops, they said.

Amazing.

According to Patrick Lynch, the head of the police bargaining unit, Garner's killer was a "model officer," an Eagle Scout, and "just doing his job."

Choking a man to death for suspicion of selling a cigarette. Real respectful, eh?

By the way, anti-lynching journalist and activist Ida B. Wells spoke of how the verb "lynch" derives from the name Col. William Lynch, who instituted hangings for alleged horse thieves, without trial or due process. Hence the terms lynching and Lynch Law.

A crusading reporter, Ida B. Wells would be amazed at how easily Blacks could be killed in the 21st century by police, without due process.

Her keen eye would survey New York, Cleveland, Ferguson, and beyond, and perhaps she would recognize modern-day Lynch Law.

FERGUSON: THE EPICENTER

For the Rosa Luxemburg Conference, Germany
January 1, 2015

For tens of thousands of young people in America, protests against police violence and state terrorism are the order of the day. They take to the streets every day, no matter the weather, in cities across the United States.

No single organization is directing this bold effort, and the role of traditional civil rights leaders is greatly diminished.

The protests are largely the work of youth using the weapon of technology to demand social justice. Their efforts are unmediated and unfiltered by the political parties. They are independent of these parties, and thus able to frame their issues in their own voices, in their own words.

Thus we see placards and hear chants such as "Hands Up! Don't Shoot!," "I Can't Breathe!," "Jail Killer Cops!," and the like.

None of this would be happening without Ferguson, Missouri. It was a stark, unblinking illustration of the repression of the armed state against Black existence, Black community, and the Black family. It also shows us how sniper rifles and automatic weapons, and even armored personal carriers (urban tanks!) will not stop or deter people who were determined to hold police accountable.

Images from Ferguson flashed around the country and the world, igniting protests in nearly 200 cities.

It broke through the illusion that had been promoted by the media and the political classes: That America was a compliant post-racial society.

It showed the impotence of Black politicians to make the lives of average Black people more secure.

Ferguson may prove to be America's Tahrir Square, the epicenter of resistance to chronic social injustice.

The wave of national protests emanating from Ferguson are a demonstration against the way police kill with naked impunity, especially when their targets are Black.

When cops kill, the system rises up to protect the killer(s), by secret grand juries, prosecutorial discretion, and when all else fails, judicial appellate protection that virtually guarantees that any conviction will be reversed.

That's what Ferguson revealed, the dirty little secret of police immunity in America today.

To a German audience, with a historical memory of terms like *Untermenschen*, the concept of state killing with impunity must be chilling.

But let us be clear: Black America, despite its glitter and pop, is an oppressed community. It is exploited economically, as in Ferguson, where a plethora of fees and fines threaten the people with debtors' prison, unless they submit to paying exorbitant court costs.

These monies support a veritable apartheid system: a primarily white, yet woefully unrepresentative, local government, coupled with the very essence of what drove the colonial rebellion against the powerful British crown: taxation without representation.

Blacks are subject to unprecedented mass incarceration nationwide which, as law scholar Michelle Alexander notes in her book, *The New Jim Crow*, closes the door to almost every other opportunity in American life.

Thrown into nonfunctional public schools, denied jobs, harassed on the streets for Walking While Black, Driving While Black, and even Talking While Black, life for millions in Black America is far too often a living hell.

It's these chronic conditions that pulled the trigger in Ferguson and launched similar mass movements nationwide.

Those movements are still going strong.

May they only grow!

BLACK LIVES MATTER?

January 22, 2015

With news emerging that the FBI will not begin proceedings against killer cop Darren Wilson in the murder of Black teenager Michael Brown of Ferguson, Missouri, we wonder: how many people are surprised?

Were his civil rights violated?

Apparently not, except for his rights to "Life, Liberty, and the Pursuit of Happiness," of course.

But for far too many Black youth, this doesn't matter.

Civil rights prosecution? Nope, not today.

Not ever.

The only thing that would've surprised us would be if there *was* a prosecution.

But we needn't have worried about that.

Recently, Sybrina Fulton, the grieving mother of Trayvon Martin, wrote a letter to the grieving mother of Mike Brown, Leslie.

She wrote:

> Further complicating this tragedy is the fact that the killer of your son is alive, known and currently free. . . . Your circle will necessarily close tighter because, the trust you once, if ever, had in "the

system" and its agents is forever changed...but with those changes come new challenges and opportunities. You will experience a swell of support from all corners of the world. . . . If they refuse to hear us, we will make them feel us. . . . We will no longer be ignored.

Mother to mother.
Son to son.
Injustice to injustice.
"Black Lives Matter"?
Not yet they don't.

FERGUSON, USA

March 5, 2015

With breathless news reports, the U.S. Justice Department's Civil Rights Division investigation of the Ferguson Police Department[34] paints a damning picture of a long, cruel, and bitter normalization of maltreatment, mass profiling, police targeting, and brutality against Black people in the Missouri town.

What may be even worse, however, is how the town's police, judges, and political leaders conspired to loot the community, by fining them into more poverty—with fines that supply approximately 25 percent of the county's budget.

Correctly, cops have been criticized for their juvenile emails and texts of racism and contempt against the local Black community and even Black leaders in Washington, D.C.

There is largely silence, however, over the role of judges, who have used their robes to squeeze money from the community, issuing unfair fines and fees—even using their jails as an illegal kind of debtor's prison.

In 1869, during the reign of England's Queen Victoria, a statute known as the Debtors Act was passed, which forever abolished imprisonment as punishment for debt.

In today's Missouri, it's still used to punish and further impoverish people in low-income communities.

But, truth be told, it ain't just Missouri.

Renowned *Rolling Stone* writer Matt Taibbi, in his 2014 book *The Divide*, tells a similar tale, but from points all across America—Brooklyn; Gainesville, Georgia; Los Angeles; San Diego, and beyond—where poor people are being squeezed by cops, judges, and local governments, to part with their last dime to finance a system that is corrupt to the core.

Taibbi's full title might give us some insight: *The Divide: American Injustice in the Age of the Wealth Gap.*

This is America's official economic system—capitalism—a system of racialized exploitation and relentless predation.

WORDS VS. DEEDS
March 11, 2015

For now, the fraternity Sigma Alpha Epsilon is perhaps the most well-known fraternity in the United States, for all the wrong reasons.

It's also been disbanded from the campus of the University of Oklahoma at Norman, for all the wrong reasons.

Despite what you may believe, it's been disbanded because it got caught on tape, and it embarrassed the university.

Period.

Consider this: a silly, racist chant among teenage college students lands several of them with immediate expulsions, and the closure of their fraternity.

In neighboring Missouri, an entire city infrastructure targets, oppresses, and leeches millions of dollars from a Black community (Ferguson)—and, lest we forget, kills them on a whim—and who gets fired?

No one.

Oh, there are some resignations, yes, but not one firing! There's a world of difference between the two.

In Oklahoma, the most powerless people on campus, the youngest, are handed the most extreme sanction: expulsions.

In Missouri, politicians and police, criminally conspired

to loot, exploit, and bleed and entire community—but not a single person gets fired.

What's worse: racist words, or racist actions that harm thousands of people for years?

The University of Oklahoma, founded in 1890, could have used this as, well, a teaching moment, about the way racism moves from one generation to the next, and how closed systems in groups perpetuate harm against their fellow Americans.

The university, while disclaiming the racism, could've used its history department to teach the roots of such social injustice in American—and Oklahoman—history. If it has an African American studies program, it could've been a time to shine, by providing a study program for members of Sigma Alpha Epsilon.

But, first and foremost, it could've defended the First Amendment principle of freedom of speech, and used the light of reason to flush out the power of racist hatred.

Instead, a 19-year-old is marked, perhaps for life, with the brand of racism, for being drunk, stupid, and mean. After the shock wears off, bitterness will fill his soul.

Colleges and universities, of all places, can't jump the gun for PR reasons. They must use opportunities to teach, to enlighten, to broaden consciousness for all students.

Even those—especially those—who love to sing about hanging niggers.

137 SHOTS
May 24, 2015

A man drives his companion down a Cleveland street, and before he knows it police sirens bite into the night air, sending a chill down his spine.

He pushes his foot down on the accelerator trying to avoid the madness. Little does he know that within minutes, he and his companion will be shown their last vision in life, 137 shots fired into them, courtesy of Cleveland's finest.

This happened in 2012, on a Saturday. A judge there acquitted a cop for leaping atop a car's hood and pumping 15 rounds from his semi-automatic into bodies of the two occupants of the car. A total of one hundred and thirty-seven bullets were fired into a car containing two unarmed people. The use of lethal force was said to have been triggered by a car's backfire.

Legal? Justifiable? The two unarmed people who were killed by police had traces of drugs in their system, the judge noted. They were thus expendable.

137 shots, it's okay, no biggie, boys will be boys, right?

The law is not but opinion, whether the judge's or anyone else's, for that matter.

In the season of Ferguson, when the youth are in the streets yelling, "Black Lives Matter," we learn that this is more aspiration than reality. It is a bitter hope in the cold kingdom of the law, for today Black lives don't matter a bit. Have they ever?

THE HERITAGE OF THE CONFEDERATE BATTLE FLAG

July 7, 2015

The current controversy over the Confederate Battle Flag fluttering over the Capitol building in Columbia, South Carolina, is a testament to many things, the least of which is whether it is a symbol of racism.

It is a measure of how backward and repressive some areas of the country are, caught in the fractured memory of the past, a past that was, for millions, far more horrific than it was glorious.

Anyone who studies American history learns that South Carolina constantly threatened to secede from the Union. Indeed, in the classic work of French political scientist Alexis de Tocqueville, *Democracy in America*, written several generations before the firing on Fort Sumter, South Carolina threatens to split from the union.

That contrariness—that sense of false, bruised pride, that deep paranoia bred into the bone because of the knowledge of centuries of crimes and cruelties waged against Africans—lies in the heart of the state, like a stone.

Of all the slave-built colonies of the South, none exceeded South Carolina for its huge, teeming population of Black families who were forced to live in terror.

That is the heritage of the Confederate Battle Flag, one of terror and violence, in the name of white supremacy and

Black subjugation, that advances a system of organized theft of Black labor, freedom, and humanity.

Dylann (*Dumb & Dumber*) Roof knew what the flag stood for, as well as the flags of apartheid South Africa and the former Rhodesia.

He knew what he was wearing and waving.

History has consigned the apartheid flags and Rhodesia's banners to the annals of the past.

But in parts of the United States, the Confederate Battle Flag flaps in the breeze as if it were still 1860.

For far too many people, the war—the Civil War—still ain't over.

AS BLACK AS THEY WERE EXPENDABLE

August 25, 2015

It's been 10 years since the watery carnage of Katrina, and one year since the fiery rage lit the night skies of Ferguson, and between the two harrowing events lay the state of Black America: isolated, demonized, and damned.

When the levees broke and the rushing waters of Hurricane Katrina swept into the neighborhoods of New Orleans, the Ninth Ward—the Blackest ward—received the greatest damage, and the least relief.

Today, 10 years after its horrific flooding, the Ninth is back to barely half of its former population of working-class and low-income inhabitants. It is but a shell of its pre-storm glory.

What the residents of the Ninth learned was the hard, cold truth that they were all on their own, alone facing the fury of the storm.

Oh, they could call 911, and they may even have gotten an answer, but no one came to help them.

For they were in the Ninth Ward, as Black as they were expendable.

Flip to Ferguson, summer of 2014, the time of Mike Brown's killing by a cop, and the subsequent explosion of protest by Black youth nationwide.

Young Black men, women, and children took to the

streets, and faced scared, paranoid white cops armed to the teeth with sniper rifles, automatic weapons, and Humvees.

How many of us know that protests have continued every day since then?

The media may've fled the story, but the people haven't. Some have pitched tents. Others have set daily times to join the protests.

But they are there, every day, to remind us of their very deep and very real discontent with an oppressive system that has soured their days and nights.

For the fires of Ferguson still burn; they burn in their hearts, they simmer in their souls, they roar in their minds.

And Katrina? If we ever wondered whether Black lives mattered, the squalid treatment of the people of New Orleans, especially the ninth Ward, answered that question decisively.

Politicians, banks, media, and entrepreneurs plucked what they could and kept on moving, leaving the intrepid souls of the Ninth to fend for themselves, isolated, demonized, damned.

Katrina and Ferguson: touchpoints for Black America.

TAMIR RICE OF CLEVELAND

October 15, 2015

Question: When is a child not a child?

Answer: When it's a Black child.

That question and answer came to me when I heard that the police killing of 12-year-old Tamir Rice of Cleveland was ruled "justified" by two so-called "independent" boards of inquiry recently.

The cop was justified, they ruled, because he saw a gun. Period.

Did it matter that the gun was a toy?

Or that Tamir was a boy?

No. Both facts were declared irrelevant.

And the life of yet another a beautiful Black child is snatched, with impunity, by the state.

What kind of system is this, where a child's life can be so easily, so utterly, evaporated?

What kind of country is this, where this can happen?

For almost a year, state forces dithered around the case. Now they have issued their cold, leaden decision:

No biggie.

The cop was scared.

It's justified.

Next.

What's next? Killing pregnant Black women who are suspected of creating more Black boys?

In the name of protocol, in the name of tradition, in the cold name of fear, Black children are killed so that white cops can feel safe.

This system is intolerable and must be abolished.

DISTURBING THE PEACE
October 28, 2015

The video is stunning.

A muscular cop leans over a skinny schoolgirl, flips the chair in which she sits, sending her on a hard fall to the floor on her back.

Before she can disentangle herself from the desk-chair, she is seized and thrown across the room, like a rag doll. She is immediately handcuffed and arrested for "disturbing" her classroom.

According to published accounts, she was said to have been a non-participant in class, and ordered to leave the classroom. When she refused to leave, the school's so-called "resource officer" was notified.

When Officer Ben Fields, a cop, arrived at the classroom, he went into Rambo mode on the girl.

The rest is infamy.

Several months ago, a video showed a mad "Robocop" assaulting a young teenage girl in a bikini.

This latest police attack on a young girl is almost identical, except that it happened in a classroom.

Consider this: the girl in the class never assaulted anyone, never threatened anyone, she merely refused to leave.

Such incidents tells us the nature of public schools, and more ominously, the nature of police. Are cops there to protect the students, or are they there as authoritarian instruments to assist the staff to discipline the students?

What is the function of teachers—to impose blind obedience, or to teach creative freedom?

Events such as these show us an ugly, unpopular, uncomfortable truth about American schools, and how they interact in the lives of children, especially Black children.

Video evidence of a beefy Black cop throwing a white teenage girl across a classroom would've evoked an immediate response.

That this has not, speaks volumes about the degraded value of the lives and well-being of Black children in America today.

BADGE OF RACISM

December 14, 2015

As the first phase of the trial of police officer Daniel Holtz-claw comes to a close, one is forced to take stock of what the trial—and the lack of media covering it—mean.

Holtzclaw, a 28-year-old white Oklahoma cop, was recently convicted of 18 charges of sexual assault, rape, sodomy, and related offenses, the targeting and raping of some 13 Black women and teenagers.

An Oklahoma jury recommended that the man be sentenced to some 260 years in prison!

If you winked, however, you would've missed it.

A serial rapist—of 13 women and teens! When isn't that a story?

When the 13 people are Black people.

Only one cable network, the Black-owned TV1 news program, hosted by former CNN contributor Roland Martin, covered the case, using Internet reports from people in court.

No one else. Not one.

Why not? Apparently, because in white America, Black lives *don't* matter.

Holtzclaw used his uniform, his badge, and his loaded gun, to stop, intimidate, and rape more than a dozen women—sometimes in his own patrol vehicle—sometimes right on a victim's front porch.

And people wonder why people in the Black community don't trust cops.

It took DNA and GPS evidence to bust this villain; but how can anyone even contemplate something so sick?

Easy. Most of the victims were Black women from low-income communities; some had been charged with being sex workers, others charged with drug violations—in other words, the most vulnerable and voiceless people!

This cop carefully chose those who he knew had no social power and little ability to resist.

And media silence reinforced his narrative by belittling the worth of these American women.

If they had covered these crimes and valued the dignity of the victims, they would've cast a harsh national light on the culture of police authority and impunity.

They chose not to.

Like a cop standing over a body in the road, they essentially said, "Keep moving. There's nothing to see here . . . keep it moving."

Have Black lives ever mattered?

BECAUSE HE IS A BLACK CHILD

December 28, 2015

The nightly news mentions in passing that Cleveland officials will file no charges against the police officer who killed 12-year-old child, Tamir Rice.

There is something shattering about the death—the killing—of a child.

When a child dies, the natural order is torn; the stars weep, and the earth quakes.

We have become so accustomed to the atrocities of this system that we are lured to accept them as natural, instead of as intolerable, and preventable, human impositions. Politicians, in the pocket of so-called police unions, bow before bags of silver and blink away the death of a child, especially if a Black child.

What man-made institution is worth more than the life of a child?

What job?

What profession?

What office?

What state?

When a child dies, adults don't deserve to breathe their stolen air.

When a child dies, the living must not rest until they have purged the poison that dared harm such a soul.

When a child dies, time runs backward and attempts to right such a wrong.

Such acts challenge our very humanity, and should inspire movements worldwide to fight like never before.

For something vile has happened before our eyes.

A child has been killed; and in America, because he is a Black child, it means next to nothing.

KILLED BY COPS WHO WERE "JUST DOING THEIR JOBS"

July 7, 2016

And now comes another.

Alton Sterling, father, husband, beloved of his family and friends, joins a tragic train of death: Mike Brown, Rekiah Boyd, Eric Garner, Sandra Bland, Tamir Rice, and on, and on, and on, and on. All killed by cops who were "just doing their jobs."

At times like these, elections seem irrelevant. For they have no answer to this gnawing state of terror. No answer at all. Why should they? They were architects of it. They campaigned for these killers. They approved their militarization, arming them with weapons of war.

The politicians running for (or running *from*) office today were gung ho for cops yesterday, sending them more and more of the people's tax dollars, as well as more and more military weapons.

What did they expect?

And within hours of Sterling's killing, another Black man—Philando Castile—was gunned down in the front seat of his car (as his lover watched in horror), while reaching for the ID and registration that a traffic cop demanded him to hand over.

Another one gone . . . and another . . . and another.

WHAT HAPPENS TO A DREAM DEFERRED?

July 10, 2016

The events of last week continue to reverberate throughout national consciousness.

The unprovoked killings by cops in the streets of America's Midwest, and the subsequent killings of cops in Texas, show us that a new stage has been reached in America's longest war with itself.

When Rev. Dr. Martin Luther King Jr. led anti-segregation protests in Selma, Alabama, in the 1960s, cops didn't "assist" protesters; they beat them, savagely, for violating the unjust laws of white supremacy. They beat men and women, indiscriminately, to protect white privilege. The Edmund Pettus Bridge became slick with Black blood.

Today, the institutional descendants of white slave patrols kill Black people of all ages with utter impunity. Prosecutors direct grand juries to defend cops who kill; not-so-secret judges repeatedly rule "justifiable homicide"; and killer cops get off free, time and time again, simply by claiming self-defense. Indeed, the U.S. justice system perpetuates immunity for police by maintaining the loophole of self-defense.

"Good job," and then nothing.

Today, media, politicians, and police all call the Texas

shooter, Micah Xavier Johnson, a madman; one prominent politician calls him "deranged."

But if he is mentally disturbed, what made him so?

Was he mad when he went to kill Afghanis on behalf of the shrinking U.S. Empire? Perhaps they trained him far too well.

Oppression can drive people mad. It can turn calm brains into minds consumed by anger, rage, and resentment.

The media, ministers, and politicians will call him names, but he is beyond your curses now.

His life was a curse already, to be born a nigger in America. That's curse enough.

In 1951, the great poet, Langston Hughes wrote in his poem "Harlem":

> *What happens to a dream deferred?*
> *Does it dry up*
> *like a raisin in the sun?*
> *Or fester like a sore—*
> *And then run?*
> *Does it stink like rotten meat?*
> *Or crust and sugar over —*
> *like a syrupy sweet?*
> *Maybe it just sags*
> *like a heavy load.*
> *Or does it explode?*

MOVE

August 1, 2016

August had barely broken its first week when police gunfire shattered the tense early morning air. It was West Philadelphia, 1978, just blocks from Drexel University.

For over a year, Philadelphia police had occupied the neighborhood of Powelton Village, under orders of the city's racist mayor, Frank L. Rizzo. Why were they there?

Ostensibly, to arrest members of the naturalist organization MOVE, allegedly for failure to obey court orders to appear.

Police were there, in Rizzo's words, to "starve them out"—to drive them from their communal home. In truth, the Philadelphia Police Department was there to kill.

The homes across from the organization's families' residence were taken over by heavily armed cops, many of whom were displaying sniper rifles and automatic weapons.

The men, women, and children living in the MOVE home endured months of terrifying psychological pressure. The area had the feel of a military occupation, complete with constant surveillance and checkpoints. People who could not produce adequate identification, for example, were denied entry to the neighborhood.

On August 8, 1978, all hell broke loose, when cops opened fire on the families across the street. The shooting forced the MOVE people to seek safety in the basement. The police responded with fire hoses in an attempt to flush them out or drown them in the process.

When MOVE members left their homes, all present were arrested. Some, like Delbert Africa, were brutally beaten, kicked, rifle-butted and then arrested.

All nine people were charged with killing one cop.

From that point to this, MOVE members were treated like a disease.

From the preliminary hearings, to trial, and through a handful of appeals, MOVE members have been judicially assaulted, denied every alleged constitutional right. From the right of self-representation to the right to a fair judge to the right to sentencing, and beyond, all MOVE members have ever heard is: "No!"

The judge who presided over the trial, Edwin Malmed, told this commentator during an on-air interview on the *Frank Ford Talk Show*, that he hadn't "the faintest idea" who killed the cop during the day-long shoot-out. "They were tried as a family; I convicted them as a family," he said.

Nine people were sentenced to 30 to 100 years.

MOVE members were, in fact, convicted for the audacity of living freely and proudly outside Philadelphia's white status quo. Thus, they were convicted for being who they were, families dedicated to the ecological naturalism of the MOVE organization.

That was their crime.

They should all be free.

BLACK LIVES DON'T MATTER

(And Neither Does Video!)
December 12, 2016

The trial of the killer cop who shot an unarmed Black man, Walter Scott, is off. Hung jury.

If the videotaped killing of Scott wasn't shock enough, the hung jury certainly suffices. The images are, to say the least, chilling,

Mr. Scott is seen fleeing in terror from a calm, younger white man. The runner appears to be one unaccustomed to running easily, yet he is running, running away from the calm-faced white man wearing a dark uniform.

As Mr. Scott runs, the calm white man pulls out a weapon, aims, and:

> pulls the trigger,
> pulls the trigger,
> pulls the trigger,
> pulls the trigger,
> pulls the trigger,
> pulls the trigger,
> pulls the trigger,
> pulls the trigger.

Eight bullets fly. Mr. Scott, clad in a bright green shirt, crumples to the green earth and breathes his last breath. The white cop calmly bends over and picks up a dark object with wires hanging from it, walks back to the body, and drops the object nearby. The cop looks as if he's strolling on a beach in the Bahamas, with not a care in the world.

But the video, apparently, wasn't enough, at least not to one of the jurors who refused to convict ex-cop Michael Slager despite the overwhelming evidence against him.

The murder of Mr. Walter Scott, documented on videotape for all to see, proves, if proof were needed, that Black lives don't matter, at least for that jury. And guess what? Apparently, videotape doesn't matter, when a Black person gets killed by a white cop.

Remember when MOVE member Delbert Africa, unarmed (his upper body bare), was beaten, punched, kicked, and stomped by several Philadelphia cops? A white judge dismissed the video evidence of his beating, and acquitted three cops.

LAPD's heinous beating of Rodney King, also on tape, remember? A predominantly white jury ignored the video and acquitted the cops.

The Black Lives Matter movement was called into existence, and has so much work to do, because, well, Black lives still don't matter.

TO PROTECT AND SERVE WHOM?

Published as pamphlet in September 2015, updated February 2017

What makes a movement, a *Movement*?

What social forces come together to make it cohere, to build it into something that can stand in the world, like a new-born thing, able to drop, rise on unsteady legs, breathe deeply, and then run its course?

Consider this: There has never been a time since the "founding" of the U.S. government that there has not been a movement of some sort, but, like any other thing in life, such movements have been weak or strong, in ebb or flow, depending on the social conditions from which they emerge.

We live in an era where the very notion of a movement seems strange, or out-of-time.

That may be because over the last half century, the state has worked hard to counter the influence and memory of movements as soon as possible.

The state projects itself through the institutions of media, the academy, and public schools so as to present a false, misleading historical narrative that confuses people. As a result, it becomes difficult to see a social movement grow, interact, swell, and finally, present its positions in the public square so that they cannot be easily refuted.

Thanks to movement scholars, we know of the deep hatred and venomous methods deployed against the late Rev.

Dr. Martin Luther King Jr., a man whom the U.S. government nefariously pressured to kill himself.

The Reverend's greatest enemy was his own government, a force crystallized in the person of the director of the FBI: J. Edgar Hoover.

Hoover, an unabashed racist, used his powers to try to destroy any movement that questioned the status quo. But Hoover seemed to reserve his deadliest assaults for members of Black freedom movements.

This may be perhaps best seen in the program code-named COINTELPRO, code-speak for the Counterintelligence Program operated for decades by the FBI against U.S. citizens, particularly Black movement leaders from Dr. King to Dr. Huey P. Newton of the Black Panthers. All were treated, in the words of William Sullivan, Assistant Director of the FBI, while speaking to staffers of the U.S. Senate committee investigating COINTELPRO, as enemies of the State:

> This is a common practice, rough, tough, dirty business. . . . To repeat, it is a rough, tough, dirty business, and dangerous. . . . [N]o holds were barred. We have used that technique against foreign espionage agents, and they have used it against us.
>
> Questioner: The same methods were brought home?
>
> Answer: Yes; brought home against any organization against which we were targeting. We did not differentiate. This is a rough, tough business.[35]

Nor should we forget how the FBI viewed Dr. King. Again, Assistant Director Sullivan's words: "We regard Martin Luther King as the most dangerous . . . Negro leader in the country.[36]

Why is this important to us, now, in the womb of another emerging national movement? It is vital, for it teaches young activists and revolutionaries in the making, that this is the real, essential nature of the state: militant opposition to any social force that seeks to make it more open, democratic, and accountable, and that threatens to increase public control over public resources, institutions, and affairs. If you begin a social movement and fail to understand this historical reality, you will march into a buzz saw that will leave you in pieces.

The Reason Movements Emerge

When a society reaches a dead end, when it can no longer persist in its old ways, social movements arise to push it to its next stage of development. If that social movement is able to project its ideas, and spread them widely enough, and these ideas find room in the hearts and minds of the People, such movements may make that next step, and define the era's zeitgeist and what is and is not the common good.

History shows us that social movements can transform society, but they do not go uncontested, for the status quo of the state abhors change. The state always sees change as a challenge, and it utilizes its vast power to counteract any such change.

Note well that we have been using the well-known and well-documented example of the U.S. Civil Rights

Movement to proffer these ideas. On its face, such a national movement seems benign today, for in some ways, it has succeeded in integrating its narrative and perspective into the nation's narrative and perspective, and into the hearts and minds of people around the globe. Rev. Dr. Martin Luther King Jr. is a national hero who is honored with a national holiday and a towering granite statue of his likeness on the Mall of the nation's capital. Moreover, his visage stares out from the semi-grottoed wall of the Church of England, where he is recognized as a saint.

If the state could do what it did against a mild-mannered minister such as Martin Luther King, what can it do to you?

Answer: *Whatever it wants to.*

Activism is neither easy nor necessarily safe, and that is especially so in this age where the people are exposed to an Orwellian level of internal surveillance, police militarization, and criminalization of dissent unprecedented in U.S. history. Being active in the movement to hold police accountable for their crimes against people and their communities seems only to increase exposure to such forces of intolerance.

This Movement for Justice Against Police Violence

It is no coincidence that the words "police" and "politician" are so similar, for they both derive from the same Greek term for city-state: *polis*. Police are the employed servants of the state, and as such the instruments of state policy. And what is the state? Marx and Engels said: "The executive of the modern state is but a committee for managing the common affairs of the whole bourgeoisie."[37] Thus, police serve the ownership and wealth classes of their societies, not the middling or impoverished people. For the latter, it is quite the reverse.

That's why we see the police utilized to surveil those who organize labor, the oppressed, social movements, and networks of resistance, and why they beat down those who dare to speak out and protest.

In Brazil, state authorities casually slay street children, for they are seen by shop owners and elites as a kind of public pestilence. In Iguala, Mexico, officials team up with narco-traffickers and disappear dozens of students. In China, police beat down students who demand real representation in state power. In New York, and across the country, cops coordinated surveillance and mass arrests in an attempt to criminalize the Occupy movement, and forced its supporters and their message, not just from the street, but from public view.

Police, therefore, don't only perform a public anti-crime policy; in order to serve their financial and political masters, they must also commit crimes themselves, crimes that involve violence, abuse, and thwarting basic constitutional freedoms and human rights.

When you look at a police car and see the motto "To Protect & Serve," don't be fooled. If you are a person of color, an immigrant, a person of conscience ethically compelled to protest, the armed authorities may not protect and serve *you*. And that is especially so if you live in a low-income community, a barrio, or in the darker-skinned part of town. If you are wealthy—what the Occupy Movement made infamous by calling it "the 1%"—then, yes, they protect and serve *you*.

What happens every day in economically disadvantaged neighborhoods of color would shock whites who live in better-secured middle-class neighborhoods. For the fact is, police relate to each community in a completely different posture.

Changing an institution requires knowing its origins. Therefore, activists committed to holding police accountable for chronic violence in our communities must know who the police really are, historically, and what social function they have performed; if activists are under-educated in this regard, or misinformed, they will not be able to see how best to approach and change the police as an institution. Understanding history keeps activists from accepting cheap reforms that act as institutional covers for the growing repressive powers of the police in an era of mass surveillance and open authoritarianism.

Taking the time to study and understand America's deep history is essential in order to see, anticipate, and plan for what is before us.

In the Beginning . . .

The vivid, energized eruptions of protest across some 200 U.S. cities in the wake of the monstrous grand jury decisions not to pursue criminal charges against the police who killed Michael Brown in Ferguson, Missouri, or Eric Garner in Staten Island, New York, were not the beginnings of the movement; if anything, they were just the most visible response of something that had been boiling and bubbling in the Black American psyche for generations. Similarly, the chronic injustice itself—illicit police violence and impunity—has rankled Black life in America for an equally long period of time.

If we read any traditional history of American policing, we will likely encounter tales that the American system was derived from the British effort to establish the London Metropolitan Police of 1829. This assertion is in error.

Two centuries before the institution of Scotland Yard got into the game, armed, violent police forces were operating in the United States with a specific role: to keep enslaved Blacks in bondage, to punish those who attempt to escape to freedom, and to deter Blacks from revolting against the system that enslaves, commodifies, and terrorizes them.

Originally known as "slave patrols," thousands of armed British soldiers were dispatched to Barbados to form the core of forces used to keep Africans in complete subjugation to their white oppressors. Indeed, this was their only job. Their import from the British West Indies to the British colonies in North America, circa 1696–1702, marked the introduction of what were then termed "militia tenants."

Their job, researcher Kristian Williams explains in *Enemies in Blue*, was to stop, interrogate, and punish any "stray" Africans, that is, any Black person who was not on a plantation and directly under white control. It was this racialized system that was imported from the British West Indies to their North American colonial outposts.

When the British enslavers spread from Barbados to what is today South Carolina, they brought with them more than the people they damned to a life of forced labor. They brought with them an armed system of enslavement and perpetual surveillance, a feature of all Southern slavery, but one particularly intense there so as to protect the minority whites from the massive enslaved Black population that outnumbered them from the earliest years. By 1860, the eve of the U.S. Civil War, South Carolina's population was 704,000 persons. Of that number, the Black population was 412,320, approximately 60 percent of the state total.

This massive number of brutally oppressed people required the minority of whites to bolster the role of the City Guard, South Carolina's early name for the slave patrol, and it demonstrated why the entire white male population was compelled to support institutional white supremacy over Blacks, and faced enlistment under pain of a substantial fine (some 40 shillings), for adult males.

"South Carolina passed laws restricting the slaves' ability to travel and trade, and created the Charlestown Town Watch," writes Kristian Williams.[38] "Beginning in 1671, this watch consisted of the regular constables and a rotation of six citizens. It looked for any sign of trouble—fire, Indian attacks, or slave gatherings. The laws also established a militia system, with every man between sixteen and sixty required to serve."[39]

Slave patrols were designed not just to deter Black revolt, but to suppress Black solidarity through music and culture. For example, Williams writes, among the duties of this early-created armed body were to "prevent all caballing amongst negroes, by dispersing of them when drumming or playing, and to search all negro houses for arms or other offensive weapons."[40]

Armed white supremacists, not Scotland Yard's Sherlock Holmes types, were the true Founding Fathers of America's police system; and fear of Blacks and Native Americans drove whites to add the Second Amendment to the U.S. Constitution.

Police, like slave owners, were given legal and customary immunity from anything done to Africans, whether enslaved or free.

That, too, is a fact; one we must come to terms with.

To be sure, every state wasn't South Carolina, nor was South Carolina every state. But it should be noted that this was an important feature of Southern society, one that centered on institutional white supremacy and enslavement of Blacks to generate enormous amounts of white wealth. And given the particularly American lust for wealth, we cannot ignore that the North, not to mention the so-called border states, also had a hand in the flesh markets of slavery. In 1790, New York led all Atlantic states in the number of enslaved people held, with some 21,000 people there forced to live in bondage. That same year, Pennsylvania had about a fifth of that number, but by 1820, Pennsylvania's enslaved population had mushroomed to 30,000. This, however, was roughly a fifth of the number for the average border state, such as Maryland and Kentucky.

That said, New York, the bustling economic whirlwind of the colonies and post-Revolution states, had its own history, in ways quite diverse from its sister states in the South.

New York, during the 19th century, was home to millions of European emigrants, many of whom were fighting anti-immigrant antipathy. The anti-Irish feeling of the

British elites carried well into the Atlantic states, and Irish folks were subjected to brutal and unrelenting prejudice in Philadelphia and New York. On the bottom economic and social rung of American society, they were not seriously regarded as white.

In Noel Ignatiev's groundbreaking 1995 work *How the Irish Became White*, he recounts the peculiar origins of the Philadelphia Police Department. There, Irish were involved in running battles with nativists who, deeply imbued with anti-foreigner, anti-immigrant, and anti-Catholic fervor, staged violent attacks on Irish people, and even attempted to burn down their churches. Irish folk In Pennsylvania and New York responded to such provocations as people in cities have done since Rome: they banded together, established gangs, and used their numbers, their grit, and their smarts to defend their communities. They also engaged in illegal activities to hustle money and boost local influence.

In mid-19th-century Philadelphia, one of the more notorious gangs, the Killers, used the local Moyamensing Hose fire department as a gang hangout. Its leader, a crafty Mexico War veteran named William McMullen, wanted to take the gang into politics.

This era featured the rise of the so-called Know Nothings, an anti-immigrant, nativist faction that commanded considerable national influence in politics during the 1850s.

By 1856, however, McMullen's organizing ability, skill at stuffing ballot boxes, and intimidation of political opponents resulted in his fellow gangsters opening up the mayorship to a Democrat, Richard Vaux, who returned the favor.

McMullen immediately offered six members of Moyamensing Hose (and also the Killers) jobs as cops. They were later known as "Dick Vaux's police," and became infamous for their epic brutality, especially against Black Philadelphians.

Through their public offices, they rolled back the nativists and formed a barrier against Black advancement in the City of Brotherly Love.

In many ways, today's institution of policing extends from a historical continuum that began with white supremacist slave patrols and, in cities like Philadelphia, organized gangsterism. And in those origins lie many of the defects of the present system. They remain racist; they remain conservative; and like the gangs that their grandfathers belonged to, they remain cliquish, clannish, and aggressive toward outsiders.

In 1850s-era Philadelphia, they didn't preserve the peace, or strive for justice. They started riots. Race riots.

Cops Riot Against the People

In early Philadelphia, both politicians and police saw race riots as important tools to establish dominance and "place"—as in keeping Blacks in theirs. This was especially so during mayoral election periods, when power was faced with challenges. Ignatiev writes:

> Election day saw continuous fighting between Negroes and whites, often initiated by Democratic police who feared for their jobs. Hundreds were injured, and three Negroes were killed; among

them was Octavius Catto, a prominent figure in the Afro-American community and leader of the campaign to desegregate the streetcars, shot in the back by a white man who was then ushered from the scene and out of the city by a policeman.[41]

Philadelphia was an urban hell for Blacks in Philadelphia for much of the 19th century. As in many other cities, Blacks suffered from the impact of a heavy, threatening, and repressive police presence in their everyday lives. And this wasn't only a 19th-century matter, for it continued throughout the 20th as well. Philadelphia, moreover, has been no different from the many American cities that became flashpoints for social conflict and racialized violence.

All over the country, low-income Black neighborhoods went up in anguished flames, and guess what the trigger was in virtually every case?

Summers of Fire

In 1965 and again in 1967, cities across America burned, set ablaze by Blacks who felt that the system was hopeless. Watts. Detroit. Harlem. Newark. Plainfield, New Jersey. And beyond.

In 1968, the Kerner Commission Report was published, and at its core sat the answer to this long train of angry, incendiary responses to chronic social discontent: joblessness, poor housing, disrespect from politicians, and the like. But one thing centered the report: "Almost invariably the incident that ignites disorder arises from police action. Harlem,

Watts, Newark, and Detroit—all the major outbursts of recent years—were precipitated by routine arrests of Negroes for minor offenses by white officers."[42]

The Kerner Report, published nearly 50 years ago, could have been published almost anytime since, as seen in the dark parade of events from coast to coast, from Rodney King in L.A. and Oscar Grant in Oakland, to Michael Brown in Ferguson and Eric Garner in New York City. Being able to witness police beat, abuse, and use lethal force against unarmed Brown and Black Americans on TV, computers, and mobile devices is the only new piece in the picture, for police terrorism of Black populations dates back to their genesis in slave patrols.

The recent cases of Michael Brown end Eric Garner have relit the fuse of civil activity and widespread social indignation. People nationwide are now deeply questioning the structures of policing that were previously less visible, beyond reproach, and unquestioned.

Why do police act as they do, especially with regard to Black Americans in the urban cores of cities?

Why do they continue to do so, when it clearly incurs such profound social costs?

Kristian Williams gives us some idea, writing of two specific, police operations against the African American communities in Chapel Hill and Los Angeles. Williams writes of "Operation Ready-Rock," in which, in November 1990, some 45 state police, canine units, and a militarized Special Response Team hit the 100 block of Graham Street in Chapel Hill, North Carolina, as if it were D-Day.

The cops declared de facto martial law, closing down the streets, bringing out their dogs, and raiding the neighborhood pool hall.

Residents were not allowed to leave, as cops were legally armed with a "blanket" warrant for the persons, homes, and vehicles of everybody on the block. Everybody.

But when the actual raids went down, the warrant didn't really "blanket" everyone, for only Blacks were targeted and searched, often at gunpoint; white people in the area were allowed to go their merry way.

The raid resulted in 100 detainees, 13 arrests, and zero convictions. Despite the victims' successful class-action suit, the local police continued to defend "Operation Ready-Rock."

Just a few years before the assault in Chapel Hill, cops in L.A., perhaps thinking of their Hollywood environs, went bigger, bringing in hundreds of cops, arresting some 1,500 people, taking 500 cars, all under the cool eye of LAPD Chief Daryl Gates, who launched the raid, "Operation Hammer," on South Central.

In this operation there were 1,500 arrests, resulting in 32 felony charges. After the big show, charges against 90 percent of the people were dropped.

Sociologist Randall Sheldon examined the raid and concluded: "The overall purpose was merely social control (of African-American youth) rather than a serious attempt at reducing crime."[44]

With themes similar to those of vintage Arnold Schwarzenegger flicks, it is hard to resist the impression that the state wasn't waging a form of low-intensity warfare, including psychological operations, against Black folks.

Williams tells us: "Though individually they receive just a meager portion of capitalism's benefits, the police represent both the interests and the power of the ruling class. Like managers, police control those who do the work and they actively maintain the conditions that allow for profitable exploitation."[45]

An Inside Look

Retired police chief Norm Stamper spent his entire adult life employed as a cop. He joined the police department as a young man, rose up through the ranks, and ended up heading the police departments in two major U.S. cities: San Diego and Seattle. In his 2005 book *Breaking Rank*, Stamper discusses the chronic racism he witnessed during his years of experience in cop culture:

> Simply put, white cops are afraid of black men. We don't talk about it, we pretend it doesn't exist, we claim "color blindness," we say white officers treat black men the same way they treat white men. But that's a lie. In fact, the bigger, the darker the black man the greater the fear. The African-American community knows this. Hell, most *whites* know it. Yet, even though it's a central, if not *the* defining ingredient in the makeup of police racism, white cops won't admit it to themselves, or to others.[46]

In his book, Chief Stamper shares a personal story about how, shortly after he left the police academy, his gruff sergeant told him to march into the neighborhood Black tavern, walk up to the biggest, meanest-looking Black man in the joint, and treat him in an insulting fashion.

Stamper, scared as hell, but not wanting to disappoint the old cop, mustered up his courage, and marched into the "Bucket of Blood." Before he could reach the biggest, meanest-looking Black dude in the joint, his superior rushed in, and called him off.

It was a test, he explained.

On a more serious note, Stamper recalled his academy training when another wizened geezer went "off book" to teach the young recruits an important lesson that was designed to save their lives. The trainer explained to them about the existence of the Nation of Islam, described as a "Black Muslim cult" that had pathological hatred of white people. The elder instructor warned them to be especially wary of Nation of Islam members, for they believed that white cops were "devils," and it was their duty to send them to the next world.

Stamper said that hearing such things scared him shitless.

Of course, this doesn't explain every interaction between Blacks—especially Black men—and police, but it does provide some precious insight. For when men fear, they are halfway to hate; for we hate that which evokes fear in us. And as Stamper suggests, we are loath to admit our fears. It makes us angry, for it seems unmanly. A sexist view, perhaps, but there it is.

How Black Politicians Have Failed (And How White Politicians Have Acquiesced)

As these words are written, marches and demonstrations continue to erupt all across the country. These demonstrations have caught the national Black political machinery off guard.

For many of these figures have run for, and risen to, political office, but their ties to the grassroots Black community—their voter base—are tenuous, at best. As these Black office holders most often come from the professional class, they rarely have strong backgrounds in activism.

When these Blacks enter office, they usually are most concerned with their personal, professional, and political concerns, not the suffering and injustice endured by people in impoverished communities.

This is so primarily because the media act as disciplinarians against Black politicians, who are punished if they dare challenge the status quo by speaking on behalf of the most marginalized populations in the country: the Black working class and voiceless impoverished class.

When these sectors of the country are mobilized, they can impact political races, media, and policy. However, more often than not, they are mobilized on behalf of politicians who, once installed, couldn't care less about the real life-and-death vulnerabilities of their constituencies.

Why is this so? Because, in the absence of a powerful movement, in the absence of pressure from people in the streets, members of the political class serve those with more wealth and power as a way to increase their own. Instead of serving the public interest, office holders flow toward a rancid pool of financial self-interest and self-aggrandizement.

Rather than represent the social justice needs of their communities, Black office holders seem to imitate their white colleagues who serve financial power and use the privilege of their office to build up their own bank accounts, one thousand dollars at a time.

It should also be noted that many of these Black politicians hail from low-income and working-class families, and have less resources compared to their white colleagues. This means that they may be more easily lured to take extra campaign funds and become beholden to private interests rather than to the social needs of their public communities. Doing so creates a classic conflict-of-interest scenario that prevents such office holders from taking stands that might displease their big financial donors. This renders them unable to truly serve the public interest and put in some work to improve the miserable realities of Black people: chronic impoverishment, neglected schools, neglected housing, police violence, mass incarceration, prison violence, and financial predation of low-income people and communities of color. They are thus politically compromised and ideologically isolated, for, in a state that places white wealth and security above those of other Americans, to really serve communities of color constitutes a betrayal of the status quo.

Only a social movement can build the political force required to get some traction with this ilk of Black leaders. And if that don't work—and, let's face it, it may not—then old leaders gotta be rejected, and movement-supporting and movement-conscious leaders must take the helm of power.

This is especially so when it comes to Blacks in blue, who are under intense pressure to serve the white privilege structure and worldview that continues to institutionally dominate most law enforcement and judicial systems nationwide. For Black cops, like Black politicians, function in predominantly white environments, where their opinions and objections hold less sway.

Kristian Williams, in a footnote, cites an Atlanta police chief who describes his department's bargaining unit (the so-called "union") as "not a union at all, but in fact a thinly veiled cover for [Ku Klux] Klan membership."[47]

Reforms? Or Revolutionary Changes?

In the wake of the horrendous instances of police violence against unarmed Black men and boys that ignited mass marches across the country, what is the way forward? What are leading political and civil rights voices saying in response to these chronic, and increasingly publicized violations of human rights?

The responses, to be sure, seem markedly anemic and pathetic, considering the gravity of the grievances raised by the people. In a nutshell, the proposed solutions offered by local and national (primarily Black) leaders includes the following:

- body cameras for cops,
- civilian review boards of police violence,
- opening of grand jury records.

This is, to say the least, a sad and depressing set of proposals that can barely be called reforms. They are sops to the masses, stale crumbs for pigeons.

They solve nothing, for they change nothing.

Nor are they seriously expected to, for politicians, in their thirst to be seen as doing something, grab at sound bites being offered, but change nothing, for, as the videos of police beating Rodney King show us, cameras can show a lot but still not result in anything except acquittals.

What people are demanding is a real solution, not nonsense about "body cams." Such discussions are frankly meaningless.

Decades ago, at the tail end of the fiery 1960s and chilling 1970s, Dr. Huey P. Newton, Minister of Defense of the Black Panther Party, wrote several articles proposing how we might totally transform American policing.

His articles followed years of on-the-ground organizing, demanding not "community policing," but "community control of police." The core of this concept is for police to live in the community that they are employed to police, and subject to the will of the people that they allegedly "serve."

Dr. Newton gave that idea much thought, and in a series of articles published in *The Black Panther* during February and March of 1980, he presents an alternative view of how police should be structured. We here summarize his ideas:

- Existing police departments would be abolished;
- A Citizen's Peace Force (CPF) would be established to serve local community needs;
- The persons serving on the Citizen's Peace Force would be selected per council districts, starting (part-time) at age 15, for two-year terms;

• Those chosen would be trained, but also educated in areas of urban problem solving.

Dr. Huey P. Newton's service-oriented perspective departs markedly from the increasing militaristic and authoritarian project that now animates much of police theory and law enforcement practice.

Dr. Newton also writes about the spectrum of personality profiles considered best suited for serving the community.

The personality profile of a "conscientious objector" to the military draft, for instance, would be a potentially excellent fit for service on a Citizen's Peace Force. Motivation, in general, would be screened with an emphasis on selecting service-oriented, rather than control-oriented, personality types.[48]

The central objectives of his proposal are encapsulated in three key concepts: conscription, community criteria, and civilian control. At base, he argues, the Citizen's Peace Force would also act as a militia, but one profoundly different from the police forces that exist in some 18,000 towns and communities of present-day America.

Today's Movement must be more than a Moment. It must grapple with the question of whether it is reform that is needed (body cams, etc.), or deep structural changes that speak to the present crisis facing communities across the country.

The People can—and must—build solutions to this crisis, if they but dare.

What Next?

Movements are driven by commitment, ethics, intelligence, solidarity, and passions; for without passion, the embers may dim and die.

For example, what sparked the Civil Rights Movement and kicked it into high gear?

It wasn't just Martin's magnificent oratory, as much as we lovers of words wish it were so. It wasn't just Rosa Parks defying law and custom by refusing to rise from her seat at the front of a segregated bus.

This is not to denigrate their robust and noble contributions to the Movement, but to give us insight into a larger, more salient point.

Two events gave certainty and determination to the Civil Rights and Black Liberation Movements, enshrining them into the undying hearts of millions.

They were: the terrorist murder of a 14-year-old Black boy, Emmett Till, on August 28, 1955, for whistling at a white woman in Money, Mississippi; and the September 15, 1963 terrorist bombing of 16th St. Baptist Church in Birmingham, Alabama, where four little Black girls were murdered by white supremacists.

The atrocities committed in these attacks were horrific, but they were common at the time, particularly in the South. In her autobiography, for example, Angela Y. Davis recounts that white terrorist attacks were so frequent where she was growing up that her neighborhood assumed the nickname "Dynamite Hill." "Many people assume that the bombing of the 16th Street Baptist Church was a singular event," says Davis, "but actually there were bombings and burnings all the time. When I was 11 and [my sister] Fania was 7, the church we attended, the First Congregational Church, was burned. I was a member of an interracial discussion group there, and the church was burned as a result of that group."[49] The white terrorist attacks against Black Emmett Till and the Black 16th St. Baptist Church were not unusual; what was unusual was the degree of attention they received, attention that caught the conscience of the nation.

Such violent events, and the tragic sacrifices to the demons of racism and hatred, gave martyred life to the cause, and touched those who could no longer resist the moral gravity of the Movement.

Similarly, while the Brown and Garner cases seem to have attracted the most press, the case of 12-year-old Tamir Rice, killed by a cop, has struck deep and powerful chords among people in this country and beyond.

In the middle of the last century, children fell at the hands of white supremacist and racist terrorist organizations such as the Ku Klux Klan.

Today, such children fall at the hands of cops—more often than not, the hands of white cops.

Any system that permits its children to be killed with impunity would seem to be a system in dire crisis. Something at the very core of our system—and society—is irrevocably broken and must be fixed.

Cops, armed with the awesome powers of the state, are now doing what Klansmen did several generations ago—and a new/ancient movement stirs from generations of chronic injustice, passionate indignation, and knowledge of successful insurrectional histories.

When the state permits its servants to take the life of living, breathing, growing, wondrous children, it ceases to have a reason to exist in the world. It has failed utterly.

Perhaps that is the force that fuels today's youth to fearlessly stand up against automatic weapons, armed Humvees, and sniper rifles, as have the youth of Ferguson. They are fueled by deep and moving forces that compel them to confront the state terror unleashed against them.

They yell, at the top of their lungs: "We Can't Breathe!" *We Can't Breathe!*

"Your system is choking us!"

¡Ya Basta! Enough is enough! We won't take this anymore!

When people reach this point, when they no longer fear power, they are on the road to social change and transformation.

This is their time, their hour; their Selma, their Civil Rights Movement.

In many ways, the elders have failed them.

It's time for Youth to rush the microphone—and take the stage!

Addendum

February 1, 2017

When the words of *"To Protect & Serve Whom?"* were written, Barack Obama had less than two years left to serve in the White House. Who knew what tomorrow would bring? Few dared guess that the presidency of Donald J. Trump was actually on the cusp of becoming a reality. Yet this transition doesn't diminish any of the arguments in "To Protect & Serve Whom?," or any other works presented in this volume. Instead, such arguments are deepened, made more tragic, for the 45th U.S. president is mentioned here (see "The Other Central Park Rapes"), in an unflattering light, to say the least. It's safe to assume that he will spark far more antagonism than his predecessor, Obama, who, lest we forget, chided Black Lives Matter activists for their "loud shouting" and tried to shuffle them into voting booths to support one of the co-architects of the biggest mass incarceration boom in U.S. history: Hillary Clinton. Suffice it to say, he was less than successful.

Indeed, while as president Obama may have commuted thousands of sentences, his changes were episodic, not systematic. Thus, the day he left office, he also left the horrors of mass incarceration fundamentally unchanged, and in the hands of an ultra-right-wing populist endorsed by a known domestic terrorist group, the Ku Klux Klan. Barack Obama left behind a vast machinery of repression, added to the most intrusive surveillance program on earth.

As far as the Black Lives Matter Movement is concerned, by raising their voices while under the Obama period, they established their sound integrity—and perhaps it may be seen that it's possible that they should have yelled louder. For Black Lives *Do* Matter. Now, more than ever.

NOTES

1.   David E. Stannard, *American Holocaust: The Conquest of the New World* (New York: Oxford University Press, 1993), pp. 74–75.

2.   Ibid., p. 95.

3.   George M. Stroud, *Stroud's Slave Laws, A Sketch of the Laws Relating To Slavery in the United States of America* (Baltimore: Black Classic Press, 1856, 2005), pp. 226–228.

4.   North Carolina v Mann 13 S.E. (N.C. 1829), http://plaza.ufl.edu/edale/Mann.htm.

5.   J.R. Grossman, "A Chance to Make Good: 1900–1929," in R.D.G. Kelley and Earl Lewis, eds., *A History of African Americans From 1880: To Make Our World Anew*, Vol. II (New York: Oxford University Press, 2000), p. 108.

6.   *The Historic Black Panther Party* (film audio). http://search.alexanderstreet.com/preview/work/1789563?ssotoken=anonymous. Accessed 11/23/16. From *What We Want, What We Believe*, Richmond, Vt.: Newsreel Films, 1968.

7.   John King is on death row in Texas. Shawn Berry is serving a life sentence. Lawrence Russell Brewer was executed by the state of Texas on September 21, 2011. He had no last words. www.clarkprosecutor.org/html/death/US/brewer1268.htm

8.   Paul Butler, "Brotherman: Reflections of a Reformed Prosecutor," in Ellis Cose, ed., *The Darden Dilemma: 12 Black Writers on Justice, Race, and Conflicting Loyalties* (New York: HarperPerennial, 1997), p. xii.

9.   Eric Foner, *Reconstruction: America's Unfinished Revolution 1863–1877* (New York: Harper & Row, 1988), p. 164.

10.   Ibid., p. 21.

11.   Ibid., p. 251.

12.   Ibid., p. 204.

13.   Frances Fox Piven & Richard A. Cloward, *The New Class War: Reagan's Attack on the Welfare State and Its Consequences* (New York: Pantheon Books, 1982), citing Charles A. Beard, *An Economic Interpretation of the Constitution of the United States* (Norwood, Mass.: Norwood Press, 1913).

14. *Dawson v Dodd*, No. 99-CV-2644, 1999 US Dist. LEXIS 9181, www.popperyatvin.com/Dawson.html

15. Kenneth O'Reilly, *Racial Matters: The FBI's Secret File on Black America, 1960–1972* (New York: Free Press, 1989), pp. 108–109.

16. Ibid., p. 109

17. Ibid., p. 257

18. Ibid., p. 282

19. Neil Strauss, "The Pop Life: Raging Against An Unusual Benefit Concert," *New York Times*, January 27, 2017. https://nyti.ms/2jYNgHU

20. John Quincy Adams, "Appellants, vs. Cinque, and Others, Africans, Captured in the Schooner Amistad" (speech, New York, March 1, 1841).

21. Howard Zinn, *Declarations of Independence: Cross-Examining American Ideology* (New York: Perennial, 1990), p. 247.

22. David Gonzalez, "Panama City Journal; 12 Years Later, Scars of the U.S. Invasion Remain," *New York Times*, November 3, 2001. http://nyti.ms/2hW8lCk

23. Ella Forbes, *But We Have No Country: The 1851 Christiana Pennsylvania Resistance* (Cherry Hill, N.J.: Africana Homestead Legacy Publishers, 1998), p. 134.

24. Ibid., p. 110.

25. *New Pittsburgh Courier*, February 19, 2003, pp. A1, A2.

26. Kristian Williams, *Enemies in Blue: Police and Power in America* (New York: Soft Skull Press, 2015), p. 121.

27. Maria Cramer, "Hearing set for officer in e-mail case: Used racist reference in response to Gates arrest," *Boston Globe*, December 5, 2009. https://shar.es/1DHYYP

28. Ibid.

29. Helene Cooper and Abby Goodnough, "Over Beers, No Apologies, but Plans to Have Lunch," *New York Times*, July 30, 2009. http://nyti.ms/2bN0att

30. Douglas A. Blackmon, *Slavery by Another Name: The Re-Enslavement of Black Americans from the Civil War to World War II* (New York: Anchor, 2009), p. 55.

31. Lindsey Gruson, "Philadelphia Gets an Inquiry Panel," *New York Times*, May 23, 1985. http://nyti.ms/2igK6Pg

32. Manning Marable, *The Great Wells of Democracy: The Meaning of Race in American Life* (New York: Basic Civitas Books, 2003), p. 205.

33. Jen Marlow, Martina Davis-Correla, with Troy Anthony Davis, *I Am Troy Davis* (Chicago: Haymarket Books, 2013), p. 285.

34. United States Department of Justice Civil Rights Division, *Investigation of the Ferguson Police Department*, press release, March 5, 2015. https://www.justice.gov/sites/default/files/opa/press-releases/attachments/2015/03/04/ferguson_police_department_report.pdf

35. U.S. Senate, *Hearings Before the Select Committee to Study Governmental Operations With Respect to Intelligence Operations*, Vol. 6 (1976), pp. 23–24.

36. Ibid., p. 57.

37. Karl Marx, Friedrich Engels, *The Communist Manifesto*, (Chicago: Kerr, 1998), p. 14.

38. Williams, *Enemies in Blue*, p. 50.

39. Ibid.

40. Ibid., p. 51, citing text from a 1721 S.C. law.

41. Noel Ignatiev, *How the Irish Became White* (New York: Routledge, 1995), pp. 170–171.

42. Report of the Advisory Commission on Civil Disorders (Kerner Report), March 1, 1968, p. 93.

43. Williams, p. 121.

44. Ibid., pp. 121–122.

45. Ibid., p. 195.

46. Ibid., p. 92.

47. Ibid., p. 948.

48. H.P. Newton, "A Citizen's Peace Force: A Proposal," *The Black Panther*, February 1980, pp. 3, 11-24.

49. Sarah van Gelder interview with Angela Y. Davis and Fania Davis, *Yes Magazine*, February 21, 2016. www.truth-out.org/news/item/34915-the-radical-work-of-healing-fania-and-angela-davis-on-a-new-kind-of-civil-rights-activism

ABOUT THE AUTHOR

MUMIA ABU-JAMAL is an award-winning journalist and author of two best-selling books, *Live From Death Row* and *Death Blossoms*, which address prison life from a critical and spiritual perspective. In 1981 he was elected president of the Association of Black Journalists (Philadelphia chapter). That same year he was arrested for allegedly killing a white police officer in Philadelphia. He was convicted and sentenced to death in 1982, in a process that has been described as an epic miscarriage of justice. After he had spent more than 28 years on Death Row, in 2011 his death sentence was vacated when the Supreme Court allowed to stand the decisions of four federal judges who had earlier declared his death sentence unconstitutional. He is now serving a life sentence without the possibility of parole. In spite of his three-decade imprisonment, most of which was spent in solitary confinement on Death Row, Abu-Jamal has relentlessly fought for his freedom and for his profession. From prison he has written seven books and thousands of radio commentaries (www.prisonradio.org). He holds a B.A. from Goddard College and an M.A. from California State University, Dominguez Hills. His books have sold more than 100,000 copies and have been translated into seven languages.

www.bringmumiahome.com
www.freemumia.com
www.emajonline.com